Other books by Deepak Bajaj published by Manjul

- *Be a Network Marketing Millionaire*
- *Achieve More, Succeed Faster*
- *Be a Social Media Millionaire*
- *Network Marketing in 60 Minutes*

DEEPAK BAJAJ

Motivational Speaker | Corporate Trainer | Life and Business Coach

- A social media influencer with 2.2 million followers
- Bestselling author of 4 books in 9 languages
- A coach with 20+ years of training experience in sales, leadership, business growth, corporate culture, entrepreneurship, success psychology, public speaking, team management, communication skills, etc.
- Has trained over 2 .1 million people across the globe
- Has garnered 500 million plus views on social media
- Multiple-times awardee – Best Trainer and Coach Award
- Brand representative of Entrepreneurship Cell – IIT Bombay
- International Master NLP practitioner
- A three-times TEDx and Josh Talks speaker
- A master of personal transformation, Deepak Bajaj has been on a mission to inspire and empower people to be the best they can be, for the past two decades.

Deepak's live events and online courses have been recognized globally for their remarkable and consistent results. More than two million people have already attended his training sessions. His unique training methodology and delivery style have made him a leading corporate trainer and motivational speaker. He is much sought after to conduct training sessions at annual conventions, leadership programmes, conferences, dealer meets, and other corporate events.

DREAMS TO REALITY IN 5 STEPS

Your Roadmap to Unlimited Wealth, Success and Happiness

DEEPAK BAJAJ

Manjul Publishing House

First published in India by

Manjul Publishing House

• C-16, Sector 3, Noida, Uttar Pradesh 201301, India
Website: www.manjulindia.com

Registered Office:
• 10, Nishat Colony, Bhopal 462 003 – India

Distribution Centres:
Ahmedabad, Bengaluru, Bhopal, Chennai, Hyderabad,
Kolkata, Mumbai, New Delhi, Pune

This edition first published in 2024
Third impression 2024

ISBN 978-93-5543-408-1

Printed and bound in India by Repro India Ltd.

Dedication

This book is dedicated to each one of you, who not only has dreams but also the drive and the commitment to work for those dreams.

As a common man, growing up in a village, studying in local schools, facing financial struggles, moving from job to entrepreneurship, making mistakes and starting all over again, multiple times, I have been through all of it and I know how it feels.

Trust me, you have seeds of greatness within you and this book is my contribution to bringing out the legend in you.

Now is your time to rise.

Go for your dreams.

Stay unstoppable.

Table of Contents

Introduction 11

1. Dreams 13
2. Absolute Faith 33
3. Preparation for Success 59
4. Massive Action 97
5. Ecosystem for Success on Autopilot 119

Nine Key Areas of a Good Life 145

Conclusion 173

Deepak Bajaj's Journey 177

Deepak's Services and Solutions 181

Acknowledgments 183

Introduction

I know of no more encouraging fact than the unquestionable ability of man to elevate his life by conscious endeavour.
– Henry David Thoreau

When I was a child, whenever I saw an aeroplane flying in the sky, I kept admiring it, and every cell of my body said one day I would also fly in an aeroplane. When I saw a good car passing by, I dreamt of having one for myself. When I saw people going on foreign trips, I also felt the desire to take my parents and family members on foreign trips. Nowadays, we see photos of luxury cars, private jets, and exotic vacations on Instagram and we also dream of enjoying these things someday. I very strongly believe that dreams are the very core of life and each one of us should have dreams.

In two decades of my professional career, I got an opportunity to train and work with two million plus people and one thing I found common in almost all of them is that they all have dreams. Everyone wants a better life, better health, more money, bigger cars, better lifestyle, etc. But they are not able to accomplish their dreams, because just thinking or talking about getting a bigger car will not get them that car. There is much more to accomplishing dreams than just thinking about them. This book is the complete manual that will give you a detailed, step-by-step process to make all your dreams a reality.

There are five steps to turning your dreams into a reality and seeing a dream is only the first of them. Dream is important because it sets the direction and starts the process. If you have a dream and you are committed to doing whatever it takes, then this book with give you a clear step-by-step roadmap of everything you need to think, believe, and do to convert that dream to reality.

After working with thousands of successful people from all walks of life, I have broken down the dream accomplishment process into a simple, duplicable model that anyone can use to convert their dreams to reality in five steps. It is simple to understand, easy to implement, and can be used by anyone for any dream. So, be it a dream of success in your entrepreneurial venture, getting a job promotion, be it a dream to get good grades in school, lose weight or achieve big success in your professional career, whatever your dream is, you can use this proven model to make that dream into a reality. No tall stories or motivational speeches. This book is full of proven models and instantly implementable strategies that you can start using immediately to convert your dreams into reality.

One really special thing about this five-step model is that not only does it ensure that you will achieve all your dreams, but also that you achieve them in a way that is not stressful. It is a cosmic way to manifest your dreams into reality where you will be working throughout with the Universe's support. I wish you a brand new life and I want you to not just write your dreams, but live your dreams. And as you pursue your dreams, never forget:

It doesn't matter how many days are there in your life; what really matters is how much life you have in each of your days.

1

Dreams

Without dreams and goals, there is no living, only merely existing, and that is not why we are here.
– Mark Twain

A dream is where it all begins. Everything in this world is the fruit of somebody's dreams. Even you and me being here on this earth is a fruit of our mom and dad having a dream. From the smallest of the products and services to gigantic cities and big projects, everything is the result of someone having a dream. Even this book that you are reading right now is the result of my dream to share with you some of the wisdom and tools that I have gathered in the past three decades of working on my own dreams.

Hundreds of books have been written about the power of dreams, and every day new concepts are introduced about dreams by authors, thinkers, and trainers. I can also give you so many definitions, but my coach always tells me one thing—we as mentors and coaches have a responsibility to break down complex things into simple ideas and solutions so that we can make transformation easier and faster for everyone.

I strongly believe that dreams are the essence of life. A seed becomes a plant, and then a tree. A tiny embryo in the womb of a mother takes birth as a little infant, and grows everyday to become a toddler, child, teenager and finally an adult. The universe has always been giving us signals that life is nothing but growth. I always tell my trainees that growth is the only evidence of life. If you are not growing, you are not actually living; you are dying.

For the first few years of your life, your growth is your parent's and Universe's responsibility. But once you cross your teenage years, your growth becomes totally your responsibility. Your parents, teachers, mentors, trainers and the universe can inspire or empower you, but the responsibility will always be yours. I give the name of dreams to this responsibility to constantly grow and rise.

My grandmother used to say that there are eighty-four lakh different living beings in this world and that humans are superior to all. What makes us God's best creation is the fact that among millions of living beings on this earth, we, humans, are the only ones who have the power to dream, the power to change our destiny.

A dog, a cat or a pigeon cannot change where they live, what they do, and how they live. But we, humans, can and this is our biggest power, our biggest advantage. A man or woman can choose how they want to live their lives irrespective of the circumstances in which they were born. We are just one decision and a few actions away from a totally new life and the best part is that we can take that decision anytime we want. To me, that decision to grow is called a dream.

Every living organism eats, rests, plays, sleeps, works and dies, but we the human beings are the only ones who have this power to dream and to live a glorious life way above this ordinary living. I strongly believe that the universe or our creator wants us to grow and evolve, and that the pursuit of growth is what is the essence of being a human being. If nature did not want us to evolve, why would it give us this incredible power to dream? Growing and rising is our biggest privilege and not utilizing it, is the biggest insult to God. You have been blessed with so much talent, potential, resources and opportunities. What do you think will happen if you meet

God after your death and tell him that all the talent, power and resources that God gave you, you have brought them back untouched and wrapped? Do you think your creator will be proud of you? Definitely not.

I look at life with this one simple understanding

Dream = Growth
Growth = Life
Hence Dreaming = Living;
Not dreaming = Death

I read this quote many years back. Most of the people die at thirty. They just wait to be buried at seventy-five. When dreams die inside a person, that person is not living any more. They are just vegetating or surviving.

So wherever you are and whatever you do, whatever the set of circumstances you are currently living in, just believe that today is the first day for the rest of your life, and you can design your life the way you want. Just commit yourself that you will make the rest of your life, the best of your life. And as you feel that desire inside you, please remember God never gives you a dream without the power to achieve it. You just need to claim that power and it is yours.

If you never dream, you will never know the endless possibilities of what you can become.
– Annette White

When Dreams are so amazing, why are many people scared of dreams, or why do people just settle for a mediocre life?

Many people lose faith in dreams because they have tried a few times and never got what they wanted. There were multiple reasons why they have not achieved their dream, but they have somehow accepted the wrong belief that they cannot achieve their dreams. There are many others who feel that the dream will bring struggle and challenge, so why not comfortably just be wherever we are and enjoy life?

As a child, we all had a big list of desires, and we all wanted to get something, do something or be something. We did not have any limits on our dreams, and we genuinely believed that everything was possible. But as we moved ahead, our schools, colleges, relatives and our environment weakened our faith in ourselves and strengthened a wrong belief that dreams do not come true. We gave up our powers and stopped dreaming. We just learnt how to follow the crowd.

As per biology, skills that are not used become obsolete or less functional. If you don't use your legs, they get weaker by the day; if you don't use your arms, they automatically get weaker. Since most people have not used their dreaming power for long, it has become obsolete for them. I want to remind you of your infinite powers, and reignite that fire in you to accomplish any dream you want. Do you remember how many times you fell before you learned to walk? You crawled for months, you took the help of a table or a bed to stand, and it took you hundreds of attempts. Then one day, you could stand without any support. It took you hundreds of falls to walk just a few feet. There were people around you watching you fall. You failed repeatedly, but every time you just bounced back. You never bothered about what others were thinking. You had this dream to walk, and you just did not rest till you could walk.

Show me one person who has not fallen multiple times before learning how to ride a bicycle. We all fell and fell again and then again. But our desire to ride that cycle was so strong that we never cared about failure, disappointment, number of failed attempts or ridicule by others. We fell and got up instantly. It did not even register in our heads that unsuccessful attempts had anything to do with failures. We just continued. Falling was just a natural step to riding a cycle.

If any of you have learnt a musical instrument or professional dancing, you know how many thousands of attempts have to happen to get that one perfect note or one perfect move.

But what happened to us now? Where have we lost our appetite to try new things, and be persistent about learning a new skill or activity? When did we start putting so many conditions to call ourselves a success? Why have we started defining every attempt as a success or a failure? An attempt is an attempt. You will get it eventually, but why quit? I just want to tell you that you started off right in your life. But on the way, you lost track and got some wrong assumptions that appeared harmless and came from people who seemed to care about us. Eventually, those safety nets became our very limits.

Reclaim the powers that you used to learn walking, talking, cycling, learning ABC and whatnot. Re-examine how you define success or failure. Redefine the meaning you give to your attempts. And reclaim your power to dream.

A car is safe in the garage, but that is not what it is made for. A ship is safe in the harbour, but that is not what it is made for. A shoe is safe in the shoe box inside your cupboard, but that is not what it is made for. In the same way, human beings may also appear safe in their current comfort zones, but that is not what we are here for. We are here to explore possibilities and grab opportunities to unleash our highest potential. We are here to create something that even goes beyond us. We are here to scale newer heights that surprise us and the world, and to inspire the coming generations to do more and be more.

As Deepak Chopra says, '*Success in life can be defined as the continued expansion of happiness and progressive realization of worthy goals.*'

If you think dreams bring stress to your life, I would like to bring to your kind attention that stress is not bad. There have been studies that prove that some amount of stress is key to a long and healthy life. After observing a group of test subjects for more than twenty years, Dr Howard S Friedman, a psychology professor at the University of California, Riverside, discovered that people who maintained a low level of stress, who faced challenges and put their heart and soul into their work to succeed, lived longer than those who chose a more relaxed lifestyle and retired earlier.

The future belongs to those who believe in the beauty of their dreams.

– Eleanor Roosevelt

Here are some insights I have had about dreams, being closely associated with them for three decades.

Don't set dreams to impress others. Set dreams to express yourself

Don't dream of buying a car because everyone in your circle would love that car. Don't talk about achieving that rank or house or foreign vacation just because it is cool or popular. Have a dream that is close to your heart and that brings out the best in you. Have a dream that wakes you up with a spark in your eyes every morning and nudges you to work endlessly in the pursuit of that dream.

When the motivation or drive to do something or achieve something is based on extrinsic factors, it is short-lived, but when the drive to achieve something is intrinsic, it gives you passion, strength, and deep fulfilment on your journey to achieve it. Every dream will demand hard work, commitment, sacrifices, and extended hours of work, and nobody can sustain it for long just to impress other people. Please remember: Doing something that you don't want to do is called stress and doing something that you love is called passion. So let your dream be an opportunity to explore who you can be and what you can achieve. Let your dream be the catalyst to express your hidden potential.

It is not just about how big your dreams are, but how long you can keep your dreams alive.

Everyone talks about big dreams as it has become fashionable to talk big. But if you study the success stories of founders of Apple, Meta, Amazon, Reliance, Alibaba, Infosys or Google, you will understand that these organizations have scaled heights way bigger than what their founders had originally dreamt. All the founder had, was an idea and a vision of where that idea could go. This vision was based on their existing knowledge and market conditions. They worked on the idea with full faith and overcame all challenges. As they achieved one milestone after the other, the dream continued to expand. Looking back, it seems what they have achieved is infinitely bigger than what they originally dreamt of. So essentially the game is not just about dreaming big, but about keeping that dream alive despite all the setbacks and challenges and letting the dream expand with every victory.

Love what you do and do what you love.
Don't listen to anyone else who tells you not to do it.
You do what you want, what you love.
Imagination should be the centre of your life.

–Ray Bradbury

Don't let your relatives or friends talk you out of your dreams

As a big dreamer, you have a responsibility to safeguard your dreams in the midst of a tsunami of contrary opinions. You may not believe it if I say that most of your relatives and friends don't really want you to achieve anything big in your life. They very well understand that if you dream big and if you act on your dreams, you will be a bigger and a better person. Then you may seek better friends, move out to a better location, and seek better standards in life. Unfortunately, your old friends and relatives may not fit in those standards. In such a situation, they will have only two choices; either to level up or get out of your friend list. Levelling up will be too uncomfortable for them. So they find a better strategy of hypnotizing you into believing that dreaming big is a waste of your time and energy. They will continue giving you stories and evidence until you decide to stay small and stay the same.

Sometimes, I feel that your low-dreaming friends or relatives have been planted by God in your life to test your commitment towards your dreams. I know it is tough, but you have to go through with it. Also, if you find yourself in such a situation, don't even try to convince them to see your point of view. It will never happen. Instead, focus all your time and energy on pursuing your dream, and just keep going.

Scan the link on this page and you can watch a special video I made on what would happen when you start dreaming big, and how to handle that dream. The title of the video is *Mere guru ki char batein jinhon ne meri zindagi badal di.* You can access this video on my YouTube channel – **Deepak Bajaj.**

YouTube Video - 4 things I learnt from my Guru

Remember, your friends and relatives definitely want you to do better in life. But they never want you to become better than them.

To be a human being is to be in a state of tension between your appetites and your dreams, and the social realities around you and your obligations to your fellow man.

– John Updike

Set a new bigger dream as you approach the completion of the previous one

What does the accomplishment of a dream do for you? As you achieve one dream, it expands your belief about what can you achieve. Also, the journey of accomplishing a dream enhances your confidence and multiplies your skills. The journey of overcoming obstacles to accomplish your dreams also strengthens your emotional mastery. So, any time when you are about to accomplish a dream, with these new beliefs, confidence and skills, you should aim for something bigger, higher or better. As you approach the accomplishment of one dream, it is time not to settle; it is time to soar higher and set a bigger dream.

Look at the photos below–Amitabh Bachchan, Jeff Bezos, Mark Zuckerberg, Narayan Murthy, Narender Modi, Ronaldo and Mukesh Ambani. All these people have way more fame, influence, and wealth than any one of us, but still, these people are working harder today than ever before. What makes them work so hard? Their dreams.

If all these people are still working hard after achieving massive success, wealth & fame, What's your excuse?

My guruji always tells me that the question is not from where to here; the real question is from here to where. Always remember that if you can achieve your current level of success starting from zero, just imagine where can you reach with your current set of skills, confidence, and experience. Imagine how many more lives you can impact with your experience and vision.

Never work on more than three key dreams at any point in time

All of us have multiple dreams, and we genuinely want to accomplish all of them. That is fantastic. Never abandon any of your dreams. We have one life; let us fulfil every dream of ours. But also remember that accomplishing every dream needs intense focus, time, and resources. After trying several combinations, I have realized that we cannot effectively work on more than three big dreams at any point in time. Once one dream is achieved, then pick up one more and continue achieving them one after the other.

I, personally, follow this simple three-step process to finalize my top three dreams

1. I make a list of all my dreams. Big list of everything I want to achieve.
2. From this list, I identify three non-negotiable dreams that will give me the highest level of success and fulfilment.
3. After identifying those three dreams I ask myself this simple question, 'If I achieve these three dreams, will I consider my life to be well lived?' If my answer is an absolute yes, I forget about all other dreams and channel my energy into achieving these three dreams.

Some of you may feel disappointed because I asked you to cut down on your big list. But trust me, achieving three big goals is far better than not achieving any one. Focus is the new currency. When you focus wholeheartedly on one thing, your chances of accomplishing that multiply manifolds. I had written a chapter in my 4th book: Ordinary People With Extraordinary Focus Can Accomplish Extraordinary Achievements.

Successful people know they need to get many things done, and done effectively. Therefore, they concentrate their time and energy on doing one thing at a time, and on doing first things first.

– Peter Drucker

Satisfaction is an excuse given by slackers

Never use your current achievements or satisfaction derived from them as an excuse for not growing further. Always be grateful for what you have achieved and continue working on the next level of accomplishments. We all have seeds of greatness inside us and dreams give us the opportunity to bring out those seeds and live our greatest potential.

More money need not be a dream for all for all the time

Money is good. We all need money to live a good life. But the decision about how much money you need specifically to live a good life is to be made only by you. I even recommend that you have our own definition of a good life. We all are unique and we must appreciate and celebrate our uniqueness. If all your relatives and friends love a luxury car, but you prefer to travel more instead of spending on a car, it is absolutely fine. It is your life and you need to define the meaning of a good life for yourself. You need to define your values and what really excites you. Time and again, I have seen that the happiest people in this world are the ones who have these two things in their lives:

1. They have their own clear definition of success.
2. They have designed their lives and daily schedules in total alignment with this definition.

So define what success means to you and continue pursuing higher dimensions of your own definition of success.

Breakthrough goals

The greatest danger for any man is not setting a high target and failing it, but setting a low target and achieving it.
– Michelangelo

Personally, for me, this concept of breakthrough goals has helped me the most in living a truly remarkable life. Working with breakthrough goals has given me the key to everlasting happiness, ever-growing impact, deep fulfilment, and spiritual connection to the divine consciousness. I encourage you also to set one breakthrough goal, and devote yourself wholeheartedly in the pursuit of the same.

A breakthrough goal is such a big goal that once you achieve it, it will totally change the pedestal from where you operate your life. It is so big that once you achieve it, you will be a different person altogether, living a totally new life. It will radically expand who you are, what you do, and how you do it. It will change your mindset, beliefs, vision, and competency. A breakthrough goal is one where you don't set a goal for incremental progress. Rather, you aim for explosive growth in a short duration of time and you aim to do something that you have never done before.

When you devote yourself to the pursuit of a breakthrough goal, what's most important is not what you get but what you become in the process of achieving that goal. By the very definition, a breakthrough goal is something that you cannot achieve by working with your current mindset, skills, and strategies. So, if you really want to achieve that goal, you need to radically expand your current level of mindset, values, skills, and working systems. You need to practically become a brand-new person and this transformation will be the greatest reward of working towards a breakthrough goal.

Imagine working on a breakthrough goal every one or two years. What will you become in over a decade? So, stop worrying about new versions of the iPhone or BMW. Get busy working on the next version of you. Does it not sound exciting? Go for it now.

Create the highest, grandest vision possible for your life because you become what you believe.

– Oprah Winfrey

You can use the questions on the next page to define your dreams and to set your breakthrough goals. You can get your copy of the exclusive **Dreams to Reality in 5 Steps – Journal & Workbook** that has all the printed forms and exercises to complete five steps to convert dreams into reality. You can order it on my website www.deepakbajaj.biz.

One of the things that can help you dream big and take consistent action on your dreams is to have an empowering power group. I have discussed about the same in the fifth chapter. There are many activities throughout this book to empower you to continuously set big dreams and to work towards your dreams. I have tried my best to give you solutions for all the obstacles that you could face in the pursuit of your dream. Don't just read this book, but also do the activities to multiply the value you will get from this book, and become capable of converting your dreams to reality.

This life is God's gift to us and how we live everyday is our gift to God. Make sure you are proud of the gift that you give to God.

– Deepak Bajaj

Key Lessons from Chapter 1 That You Should Never Forget

- Growing continuously is our biggest privilege as well as our duty. If we are not growing, we are dying and dreams are our ladder to growth.
- Most of the people die at Thirty. They just wait to be buried at seventy-five. When the dream dies inside a person, that person is not living any more. He or she is just vegetating or surviving.
- Redefine your definition of failure. When you move forward in the pursuit of your goals, there are no failures, just different attempts. Keep learning and continue moving forward.
- A ship is safe in the harbour and a car is safe in the garage. But that is not what they are made for. Likewise, we may feel safe in our current situation. But that is not what we are made for. We are made to rise, grow and scale new heights.
- Don't set dreams to impress others. Set dreams to express yourself.
- It is not just about how big are your dreams. It is more about how long you can keep your dreams alive.
- The happiest people are the ones who have their own very clear definition of success and who have designed their lives in total alignment with this definition.
- Breakthrough goals are goals that are so big that you just cannot achieve them by operating with your current set of mindset, skills, and tools. So, when you set such goals and commit yourself to the pursuit of such goals, the greatest reward is not what you get but what you become in the pursuit of achieving those goals.

Exercises to Strengthen Your Learnings from Chapter 1

1. Make a list of all your dreams. Everything you want to achieve in all key areas of your life should be put on this big list.
2. From this big list, identify three non-negotiable dreams that you believe will give you the highest level of success and fulfilment.
3. After selecting these three goals, ask yourself this simple question, 'If I achieve these three goals, will I consider my life to be a life well lived?' If your answer is an absolute yes, forget about all other goals and put your life into achieving these three goals.
4. For each of the three goals that you have just set, ask yourself why you want to achieve that goal and what will you get as a result of accomplishing that goal. Work on those goals that ignite your passion, and make you want to wake up in the morning and go to work.
5. Set one breakthrough goal for yourself. Think bigger than ever before, cross your limits, and set this breakthrough goal with absolute faith that you can achieve anything you want.

Detailed forms to complete these exercises are available in **Dream to Reality in 5 Steps – Journal & Workbook.**
You can get this from my website www.deepakbajaj.biz or by scanning the QR Code alongside.

2

Absolute Faith

Faith is the biggest force that empowers you to continue moving forward despite all failures, rejections, ridicule and setbacks.

– Deepak Bajaj

If you believe that everything begins with a dream, you are absolutely right. Everything definitely begins with a dream. But you don't want it to be only a wishful thought. Rather you want your dream to be a reality. What makes your dream a reality is a focused and consistent action in the pursuit of your dream, and you will take that action only when you have this absolute faith that you actually deserve those dreams and you will accomplish those dreams.

Anytime a dream strikes us, the first thing most of us will do is to think about the finer details that could make that dream come true. Almost immediately we start worrying about how we could arrange the money and the time to work on that dream, how would you find the right people, family support, and multiple resources that we might need for the fulfilment of that dream. Within minutes we start finding that dream too difficult to achieve, and most of us just drop that dream right there, and get busy with the same old life that you have been living. What started as a spark in our eyes and glow on our faces just vanished leaving us feeling sad and unfortunate.

This is the very moment when I want you to instantly touch your heart, look up at the sky and reach out to a feeling of absolute faith deep inside your heart. Quickly ask yourself why you have been chosen for this particular dream or desire and not anybody else. Why you and why now? Remember God never gives you a dream without the power to achieve it. Just accept that now it is your time and it is your turn, and own that dream. This is the pivotal moment when dreams become just dust for most people, but I want you to be aware of it, and overcome this.

When I ask you to have faith, I don't expect you to clearly see and believe all the details of how and when you will achieve your dream. I just want you to have this deep conviction that your dream will definitely become a reality, and let the universe handle the details. Timings, money, methodology, team, resources and all other finer details will automatically reveal themselves as you take one step after the other in the direction of your dreams.

Just take the first step forward with this confidence that you will be able to handle everything that comes in the way as and when it appears. Yes, you don't have all the skills, team, and resources right now at your disposal, but have this deep faith inside you that you will find them as you go along. Actually, you don't need all of these at the moment when you take your first step. Everything that you need to take the first step forward is always there with you. So take the first step with faith. What is the worst that can happen? You might not accomplish the dream and you might stay where you are. That is where you are right now, anyway. So you have nothing to lose, only things to gain.

The biggest victory is in taking the first step. Start from wherever you are and whatever you have. Just go as far as you can see, with this absolute faith that once you reach there, God will show you the next step.

– Deepak Bajaj

You only need so much faith that empowers you to confidently take that first step. And please remember that when you take a step forward you will have a wonderful mixed feeling of a combination of the excitement of achieving your dream, gratitude for getting the new opportunity, the adventure of trying new things, the nervousness of how it would turn out and the uncertainty of what would await you at the next turn.

As you continue the journey, you will keep navigating from one feeling to another. That is totally fine as long as you don't stop. You can even stop for a while. That is fine too. Just make sure it is only a break and not the end. I have given these five emotions an acronym of ANGEL. I have explained that in the diagram below. Just remember that as you take one step after the other, ANGEL will walk along with you.

What emotion each of us would feel and at what intensity varies from person to person. Never compare yourself to others. Just celebrate your uniqueness and your unique journey. You can either make this a difficult and terrifying journey, or a celebration of getting your prayers answered by the Universe.

Believe deep down in your heart that you're destined to do great things.
– Joe Paterno

What I am going to propose in the next line may be discarded by most people as being impractical. Nevertheless, I have realized it to be true after training more than two million people in the past two decades. If we have the slightest desire to actually make our dreams a reality, we should fall in love and learn to stay with these mixed emotions of confidence, excitement, nervousness, and uncertainty. Don't waste your precious time and energy to get rid of the nervousness and uncertainty. Just learn to manage it and navigate with this.

I don't know who started this and when it started at all. But we have been repeatedly indoctrinated into believing that we should never feel unhappy, nervous, or uncertain. It is a wrong assumption that we accept without questioning. We are human beings and we will go through all kinds of feelings and emotions. The problem is not the feeling or situation. The problem is the meaning that we give to those emotions and how we allow them to affect our life and work.

Trust me, it's natural to for anyone to feel fear and nervousness. Fundamentally, a dream is about achieving something that you have never had, and that will naturally require thinking, strategizing and doing what you have never done before. And anyone would feel the fear when it comes to doing something that he or she has never done before. Accept that feeling. Many times, fear is a signal from your subconsciousness or universe to be more careful or to prepare more. Why do you not drive on the wrong side of the road? Why do you not break traffic rules? Why do you not jump from a building? The answer is fear. You are fearful that you will die if you do any of these. Fear keeps you safe and sane.

Courage is not the lack of fear. It is acting in spite of it.
– Mark Twain

Fear is not bad as long as it does not paralyze you into inaction. Fear will never go away, so don't even try that. Let fear be with you by your side as you continue putting one step after the other. Do you think a soldier on the border does not feel fear when he or she goes to fight? Of course, soldiers do feel fear. But they do their duty, and don't let this one emotion of fear interfere with their decision-making and rightful action.

I have no embarrassment in accepting that even after training two million people and having done thousands of events in the last two decades, even today, I feel a slight nervousness for the first few seconds on the stage. Yes, I do. But that doesn't stop me from delivering training workshops to more and more people every day, and I am sure till my last breath, I will continue my life mission of inspiring and transforming people to be the best they can be.

Do it even if you are scared. Do it even if you are shivering. Do it when your mood is off. Do it even when you don't feel like doing it, but just do it.

– Deepak Bajaj

Have you ever realized what gives you the thrill on a roller-coaster ride in theme parks? It is the beautiful combination of fear and faith working together. As you are about to ride down that sudden fall, you get these tiny moments of fear that you might fall. But almost instantly you realize that nobody has ever fallen from a roller-coaster, and you have a seat belt on, and all other safety precautions in place.

Whenever you go on the roller coaster again, even though you already have this faith in your mind that nothing ever happened to you in the last so many years of going on roller-coaster rides, still that fear doesn't go away. Still, you feel those tiny moments of fear before you board the roller-coaster or when it is about to go into that deep sudden fall. It is this beautiful orchestra of fear and faith that makes this whole roller-coaster ride so thrilling and so enjoyable.

I may sound philosophical, but more than four decades of my time on this beautiful planet has taught me repeatedly that life is nothing more than a roller coaster ride and you have already boarded the roller-coaster. You will face highs, lows, sudden falls, high speed, pauses and many twists and turns. Everyone faces them. The only choice you have is how you choose to go through this ride called life. Let those moments of faith and fear come and go, you just focus on taking the next step and celebrate your journey at every step. And trust me when you are towards the end of this roller-coaster ride, you would be proud of how you made it through all those twists and turns.

The Triangle of Faith

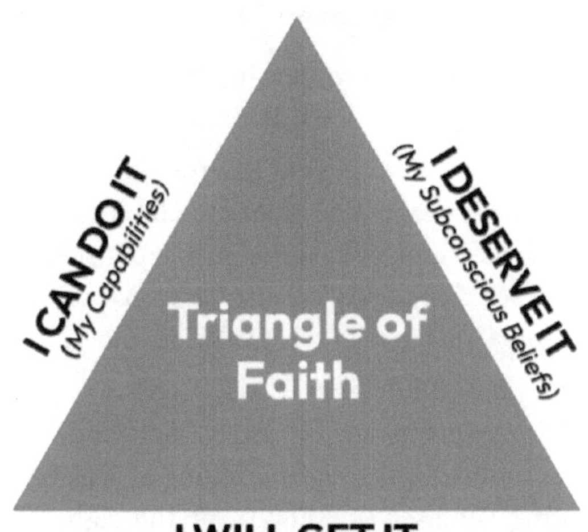

Faith has been there ever since humans walked on this Earth. Countless thinkers, authors, and leaders have given several meanings and definitions to faith. In my experience, there are three different domains of faith that work together to create the magic that is called faith, which can move mountains. When these three components are together, you practically become a manifestation factory that can bring any dream to reality. You don't work anymore; you just celebrate life every day and the cosmic power of the universe works through you to make every dream a reality. When these three domains combine, they become the most powerful force on earth, which I call the Triangle of Faith.

1. I deserve it
2. I can do it
3. I will get it

Let us discuss each of these critical elements one by one.

The First Domain of Faith – I Deserve It

How can you ever achieve something if deep inside your heart you feel that you actually don't deserve it?

A countless number of people write down their dream of earning a monthly income of rupees ten lakhs. But when they are alone and they think of that dream, deep inside themselves, they hear a voice that says, *'It is ok to write ten lakhs, but I don't think I can ever get that. If everything goes as planned, I may probably manage to reach two lakhs.'*

The same happens with those trainers and coaches who are not able to charge the right amount of fees because they start doubting themselves. They print the right fees on the brochure but keep discounting it because deep inside them, they don't believe they are worth the amount that they are charging.

If some of you struggle to sell your product or service, you may say that you are an introvert, or you don't like selling, or you don't want to overpromote yourself, etc. But if you dig deeper, probably the root cause for this problem is your internal doubts.

When you absolutely and totally believe that you deserve a higher fee, a better rank, or a bigger position, you talk differently, you act differently, and you make a way for yourself to get what you deserve.

When I talk about deserving something, I mean that your subconscious and conscious mind are in alignment with your dreams and you are as certain about getting what you want as you are certain about the Sun rising every morning. Doubts and negative self-talk are the silent killers of your dreams.

Doubt kills more dreams than lack of creativity or capabilities.
– Deepak Bajaj

Let me give an example. I have a beautiful Ferrari car, which is one of the fastest cars in the world. I am travelling to the USA for two weeks for my training sessions and business collaborations. One of my friends always wanted to drive this Ferrari. So I thought of giving this Ferrari to my friend, while I am in the USA. I called my friend and said, '*Since I am not in India, why don't you use my Ferrari for two weeks and live your dream? This is one of the fastest and finest cars in the world. You can drive it at any speed your heart desires, but just remember there is this one small problem. Its brakes don't work sometimes.*'

Now my question to you is, '*Will my friend drive this car?*' So far, I have never met anyone who wanted to go for a long drive in a car if he/she had doubts about the brakes. Please remember, the world's fastest car is useless for you if you have even the slightest doubt. How will you achieve your dreams if you are working all the time with doubts? So as you embark on this journey, I highly recommend you to kill all your doubts and make a brand-new beginning with absolute faith.

An atheist is not one who doesn't believe in God,
an atheist is one who does not believe in himself.
– Swami Vivekananda

Our life operates on faith the whole day. Do you check the driver's license of the driver every time you take a taxi? Do you check if the taxi driver is drunk or fit to drive? Do you check on the pilot of the aircraft before buying the ticket or before boarding? Have you ever met the train engine driver before rushing to board the train? No. But you put your life in the hands of all these people without any single doubt.

Do you go inside the restaurant to check if the ingredients, food quality, etc., are the same as they claim? Do you check every dose of medicine to ensure it has the required medication as listed in the dosage, before swallowing it? Do you check if the doctor has done the same replacement surgery as he promised? Do you check if the priest at the temple is saying the right mantras, or if he is even qualified to say them. No. All through the day, you put your faith in so many people for so many important things. Why then can't you believe in yourself for the accomplishment of your own dreams? Come on. Stop doubting yourself right at this moment. Ask these negative internal dialogues to shut up right now.

Ask yourself, what is the worst that can happen? You might fail? Or your plan will not work out the way you have thought? So what? Replan and restart. Learn your lessons and move forward. As a child, had you doubted yourself if you would ever be able to walk, you would have still been crawling on the ground. You did not take any classes for walking, talking or cycling. You just learnt these because you believed you deserved these and so you went for them. So whatever dream you have dreamt today, God has chosen you for this. Now for God's sake, please stop doubting God and get to work with a smile on your face.

Also, remember that your past cannot determine your future. Your past was only a learning experience. Whatever you did in the past was the best you could do in that situation, that is the best decision based on the knowledge, capability and experience that you had at that point in time. Now you are a new person with new experience, new knowledge and new capabilities. Make a new start today.

Believe in your heart that you are meant to live
a life full of passion, purpose, magic and miracles.
– Roy T. Bennett

If you want to kill doubts and negative internal dialogues, I can recommend three quick hacks that have always worked for me and lakhs of participants in my training workshop. You can also give them a shot.

1. Question Every Thought

This is an incredible idea that you should adopt as your life philosophy. Whatever comes to your mind, just question it and accept it to be true only after a thorough enquiry. We tend to believe that every thought that we get is ours, but the fact is that thoughts come to us by listening or watching or by reading someone. In most of these cases, whatever the other person has said or written is their opinion and not the absolute truth. So, question every thought that comes to your mind.

When you start questioning your doubts, fears, or limiting beliefs, they will get weakened with every question and you will realize that all your fears and doubts only haunt you till you decide to face them. When you face them and question them, they will suddenly disappear.

2. Get More Information

What is the best way to remove darkness? Light a lamp. You don't need to fight with darkness. Honestly speaking, there is no darkness. There is only light or absence of light. Similarly, wherever there is a lack of knowledge, doubts, fear, or hesitation will automatically pop up. You don't need to fight doubts or focus on them. Just get more information on those apprehensions. It is a simple formula. The amount of doubt or fear you will experience is inversely proportional to the size of knowledge that you possess on the subject. So as you stack up on more knowledge and prepare yourself well, you will see your doubts and fears vanishing.

3. Set Small Targets and Achieve Them

I have experimented with many different techniques to build and strengthen subconscious beliefs of my training workshop participants. One thing that has stood out among all the other techniques is the simple act of taking up small targets and achieving them.

This does magic. Whenever you achieve a target irrespective of its size, you give a very powerful message to your subconscious mind that you can achieve anything you put your mind to. When you do this over a period of time, your subconscious mind gets conditioned to believe that you can achieve anything and everything. As this belief gets strengthened, fears and doubts will automatically get weakened and ultimately vanish.

The Second Domain of Faith – I Can Do It

Believe in yourself, and the rest will fall into place.
Have faith in your own abilities, work hard,
and there is nothing you cannot accomplish.

– Brad Henry

Always work with this absolute faith that you have the capability to achieve your dreams. Capability is a combination of skills, knowledge, and attitude that allows any person to perform effectively, and excel in his or her chosen field. I have a deep conviction that even though you may not be a pro or top expert in your field, each one of you has enough knowledge and skills to start taking the first few steps in the direction of your dreams.

The best thing about capability is that it is never fixed and anyone can expand their capability by learning more and doing more. Have faith in yourself and in the belief that whatever it takes to begin your dream project, you have it within you right now. Top it up with your commitment to develop more capabilities as and when you need them on your journey.

I have read this amazing story about the first person who climbed Mount Everest, Tenzing Norgay. Norgay got the first opportunity to join the Everest Expedition as a porter in 1935 when he was twenty years old. For the next several years, he went on multiple expeditions with the hope of reaching the top of Mount Everest. On multiple occasions, he reached very close to the summit, but had to retreat due to some or the other difficult situation. I have read that whenever he returned to his home in the valley overlooking the Everest, he would look up at mountain and say, '*Hey you, mighty Everest, I promise that one day, I will conquer your summit because you are a rock and rocks cannot grow. But I am a human being and I can grow.*' Every time I get stuck while on a new project, or am facing an emotional low tide, I remember Norgay's profound self-belief and it just fills me up with motivation and inspiration. Finally, on 29th May 1953, after eighteen long years of relentless pursuit, Tenzing Norgay did succeed in climbing to the top of Mount Everest, along with Edmund Hillary.

You may not have the capability right now. But if you have the will to develop your capability, you are unstoppable and you can achieve anything you set your eyes on.

– Deepak Bajaj

The Third Domain of Faith – I Will Get It

Believe in your infinite potential.
Your only limitations are those you set upon yourself.
– Roy T. Bennett

This third domain in the triangle of faith is your absolute game-changer. This can turn the good into the great. This can just multiply your success and turn it into a miracle. When you start working on your goals and dreams, work with this absolute faith that the moment you start working on a dream, the entire universe also starts working for the accomplishment of your dream. Surrender your goals to the universe and let the universe handle the details about how and when your dream will become a reality.

You just focus on doing everything you can, day after day and let the Universe arrange people, places, and events for the fulfilment of your dreams. Always remember there are no accidents. Everything that is happening is part of a grand plan. No person ever rises in isolation, no dream is fulfilled without many other dreams getting fulfilled at the same time for so many other people.

Those who joyfully leave everything in God's hands,
see God's hand in everything they do.
Worries end where faith begins.
– The Bible

Always remember that life is not happening to you; life is happening for you. Every time you ask for a dream to be fulfilled, you set in motion a series of events that orchestrate people and situations to make that dream a reality. Many times, when these events happen, you may not like them, or you may feel that instead of getting closer, your dream is getting far away from you. These are the moments when you need to remind yourself that everything is happening for you and you will be able to understand the significance of current events only after a few months or years. You just become the medium, and let the universe work through you and help you manifest your dreams. Through the manifestation of your dreams, the universe will manifest the dreams of millions of other people.

My books are read by millions of people and lakhs of people have attended my live training and transformation events. Don't you think, it is not only the manifestation of my dreams alone, but also through my books or training events, the universe is actually manifesting the dreams of millions of other people as well? My trainees are the answer to my prayers and I am the answer to the prayers of my trainees. It is a beautiful orchestra that is playing constantly, and the entire Universe is working on orchestrating people, places, events, and situations for the simultaneous manifestation of millions of dreams together for millions of people.

Once you have set your goals and submitted them to God, be detached from your goals and be attached to the daily actions that you think are necessary to make those dreams a reality. This has been explained in the *Shrimad Bhagwad Geeta* as well:

Karmanye Vadhikaraste Ma Phaleshu Kadachana,
Ma Karmaphalaheturbhurma Te Sangostvakarmani

This shloka very clearly states that you have the right to work but never to its fruits. Results are dependent on many things, but actions are totally dependent on you. So, you just focus all your power on the actions at hand and let the Universe handle the details. Most people get stuck on daily details as to how and when they want the dream to be accomplished. We forget that there can be multiple ways to get from our current situation to our desired situation. Fix your goal, and be flexible and open minded about how things might turn up on the way.

As you go along, there will be modifications to the original plans and even your goal will be redefined at every stage. That is natural. In the last three decades of unstoppable pursuit of my dreams, I have personally realized that even the best ideas don't come fully formed, when they first strike us. It all begins with a faint direction. As you go along and when you experiment with different approaches and do market research on those ideas, you fine-tune your dreams and give shape to your dreams. But no one can go through this entire tedious process if he doesn't have faith in those dreams.

So, make God your partner, and along with the Universe, joyfully co-create miracles in your life.

When you start working on your dreams with absolute faith and surrender, you set in motion all the universal forces to orchestrate people, places and situations for you to achieve that dream.

– Deepak Bajaj

How Do You Strengthen Your Faith in the Universe?

1. Meditation

I have realized that meditation is a state of elevated consciousness where your attention is centred on the present moment. As your consciousness elevates, you tend to have fewer thoughts about everything happening around you and you go deeper into a thoughtless state. As you start dissociating from your current set of thoughts, you automatically start connecting deeper with the Universe. As your meditation practice deepens, you tend to get into that state faster and deeper.

During one of my training workshops, while I was asking the participants to dissociate from their current situation and thoughts, one of the participants said, '*Talking about a thoughtless state is easier to say but almost impossible to practice.*'

He said the more he tries to forget everything, the more he gets entangled in the nonstop loop of ongoing thoughts. Also, how will a ten-minute meditation benefit him throughout the day? If you also feel the same, here are my two recommendations.

First, please remember that meditation is not a goal to be achieved, it is a state to be experienced. It is not about doing. It is about being. It allows the mind to calm down and start being more aware. For the past many years, you have trained your mind to be constantly engaged in regrets of the past and plans for the future, all the time. Now, suddenly, when you want to shut everything down, it is not possible. This process takes time. So, allow yourself some time, but continue the practice.

Please don't forget that all of us are unique. So everyone's meditative state will also be different. Never make this mistake of expecting some miraculous state where you start floating in the air, or get some kind of divine glow on your face. Expectations and comparisons with others will kill the joy that meditation practice can bring. Also, start with three to five-minute sessions and gradually increase the time. You need not force yourself to increase the time, but the bliss you get in meditation will automatically increase your daily meditation time.

How do people get into the habit of drugs, alcohol or cigarettes? When people start, they smoke or drink in small quantities. As their body and mind start loving the state it delivers in those small shots, they start craving that state more and more. Over a period of time, it becomes a habit. Your body and mind have never tasted the altered state of consciousness and bliss that mediation brings to you. Once your body and mind get used to that bliss, it will automatically crave that state more and more.

As far as your difficulty in getting into a thoughtless state is concerned, let me illustrate how you can do it easily.

Imagine you got a can of mango juice and you desperately want to drink that juice. I explain to you how it is full of sugar and other preservatives and why you should not drink it. But the more I try to take it away from you, the tighter you will hold on to it. Now suddenly your mother brings the best mango shake in the world made of ripe organic mangos loaded with cashew nuts, almonds and blueberries. Now you instantly leave your juice can and grab the mango shake. How did you instantly let go of the mango juice now, for which you were so stubborn sometime back?

Leaving one thing is easier and faster when you have something bigger and better to hold on to. As you start connecting more and more with the infinite universal consciousness, all thoughts about people and events of the past and future appear so tiny and useless that you can easily drop them.

There are countless number of meditation techniques available almost everywhere. You can try some of the guided meditation available on YouTube or on several meditation apps. There is nothing wrong or right with any technique. Just experiment with a few and you will be able to find out whatever works best for you. Start your meditation journey right away and experience the bliss yourself.

True meditation is about being fully present
with everything that is, including discomfort and challenges.
It is not an escape from life.
– Craig Hamilton

2. Silent Sitting

It is actually the simplest and easiest form of meditation. Wherever you are and whenever you want, just close your eyes and be conscious of everything that is happening in your body. No need to do anything, just be conscious of it.

You can just observe your breathing as you inhale and exhale. Just observe the length and depth of your breathing. You can start counting your breathes also. It is relaxing and rejuvenating. You can do silent sitting sessions for a very short duration, say just five minutes, or can do it multiple times during the day, increasing the duration.

3. Affirmations Repetitions

Affirmations are short and simple statements about your desired state. You may or may not possess what you are saying in the affirmations. But affirmations are said in the present moment. Different authors and trainers have recommended different ways of saying your affirmations, but what I am proposing below are the basics that have worked for me and lakhs of my trainees.

I recommend that keep your affirmations short and simple. Have your own affirmation statements and not something that you write because your colleague or neighbour says so. Speak your affirmations in the present tense and the most important part is the repetition of these affirmations. My coach always tells me that repetition is the mother of all skills. It is the frequency and intensity of your affirmations that will gradually build your faith.

It is the repetition of affirmations that leads to belief.
And once that belief becomes a deep conviction,
things begin to happen.
– Muhammad Ali

Faith in Action

Some of you may wonder if faith is something invisible. If so, how will people around you notice your faith, and how it will affect your interactions with others. Faith affects your success in many different ways, both consciously and subconsciously.

Here are some of the areas where you will see faith in action

1. Your faith multiplies your confidence and confidence is a big catalyst for your success.
2. Faith brings a spark in your eyes and a glow on your face. Faith radiates a different kind of aura or vibe that reaches the subconsciousness of your prospects or clients and multiplies the chances of getting the desired outcome from the meeting.
3. When you have faith, your body language is entirely different. Your smile, posture, the way you walk, everything is just different when you have faith that whatever you have, what you are saying, and what you are doing is good for others.
4. The words you choose will also change when you have faith.
5. When you go out in the marketplace, you are bound to

face rejections, setbacks, and ridicule. Those who have absolute faith, persevere in spite of all the hardships and rejections. When you know deep in your heart that what you have is truly solving people's problems, you will find newer ways of taking it to the customers.

The dream is the seed, but this seed will become a fruit-bearing tree only when you do everything it takes to make this dream a reality. But you will take action only when you have the absolute faith that this seed has the potential to be a tree. Sometimes, I really doubt if a dream is something that propels people to action. I strongly believe that people move into action when they have faith that they deserve it and they will get it

The only thing that stands between you and your dream is the will to try and the belief that it is actually possible.

– Joel Brown

Key Lessons from Chapter 2 That You Should Never Forget

- Faith is the biggest force that empowers you to continue moving forward in spite of all failures, rejections, ridicule and setbacks.
- God never gives you a dream without the power to achieve it.
- The biggest victory is in taking the first step. Start from wherever you are and whatever you have. Just go as far as you can see with the absolute faith that once you reach there, God will show you the next step.
- Fear, nervousness, doubts and hesitation will be there all the time. Don't try to get rid of them. Just don't focus on them and concentrate all your energy on the next step.
- Remember, ANGEL will be with you at every step of your journey to your dreams. Adventure of trying new things, Nervousness of how will it turn out, Gratitude for getting the new opportunity, Excitement of achieving your dream and Uncertainty of what will await you at the next turn.
- Life is a roller coaster ride and you will face highs, lows, sudden falls, high speed, pauses and many twists and turns. Everyone faces them. The only choice you have is what meaning you give to these events and how you feel about them.
- Doubts and negative self-talk are the silent killers of your dreams.
- Three powerful keys to remove doubts and fears. Question every thought, increase your knowledge, set small targets and achieve them.
- Always remember life is not happening to you. Life is happening for you.
- Once you have set your goals, be totally detached from them and be totally attached to achieving daily process excellence.

Exercises to Strengthen Your Learnings from Chapter 2

1. Anytime you are going through negative emotions, remind yourself not to believe every thought that you get. Always tell yourself that you are not your thoughts. Practice questioning every thought.
2. Set small targets in every area of your life and do whatever it takes to achieve them. Don't focus on the size of the goal. Focus on ensuring that you do it without fail.
3. Practice meditation every day. Try different styles and techniques. Repeat whatever works best for you. Start with three to five minutes every day.
4. Create your own set of three to five affirmations in alignment with your goals and repeat them multiple times during the day.

Scan here & go directly to my website

www.deepakbajaj.biz

Detailed forms to complete these exercises are available in **Dream to Reality in 5 Steps Journal & Workbook.**
You can get this from my website www.deepakbajaj.biz or by scanning the QR Code you see alongside.

3

Preparation for Success

Willingness to live your dream life is common. Everyone has that. What is rare is the willingness to prepare and that's the biggest differentiator between those who make history and those who read history.

– Deepak Bajaj

I am a big fan of preparation and it has played a major role in whatever I have been able to achieve. Whoever you are and whatever has been your past, irrespective of your current income, rank, financial position, education, or location you can achieve anything and become anything if you are willing to prepare. This may sound like a tall claim, but trust me, if you prepare well, you can achieve anything. Yes, absolutely anything in life.

Every single time I had a new dream and I started working on any new project, big or small, I was fearful. I doubted myself and didn't have complete confidence. Honestly speaking, I face these feelings of doubt, fear and lack of confidence even now, when I start something new. But I remind myself of this one formula that brings an instant smile to my face and puts me back on track towards achieving my dream. Here is my winning formula.

Your confidence will go up and your fears and doubts will go down as you increase the level of your preparation.

Just take a firm decision to move ahead in the pursuit of your dreams with the commitment that you will confidently face whatever comes your way, using all the capabilities that you currently possess. At the same time, be open to develop new capabilities as and when you need them. Use your current team but, at the same time, be committed to bringing in new team members as and when you need them. You become unstoppable when you work with an approach that you will either find a way or make a way but you will do everything possible to continue moving towards your goal. Always remember that as long as you continue learning, growing and preparing, you can achieve just about anything.

It is simple. If you are not willing to prepare, nobody can help you; but if you are willing to prepare, nobody can stop you.

Let me give you a winning tool that will make you a lifelong winner. I call it LEAP.

You might have heard this advice regarding taking a leap of faith for your dreams. Once you associate this new meaning to the word LEAP, it might be easier for you to take that leap of faith and start action. Here is my LEAP for you to take a leap.

LEAP = Learn, Engage, Adapt, Persist

The LEAP formula is a reminder of four key activities that you should continue doing as you move forward in pursuit of your dream.

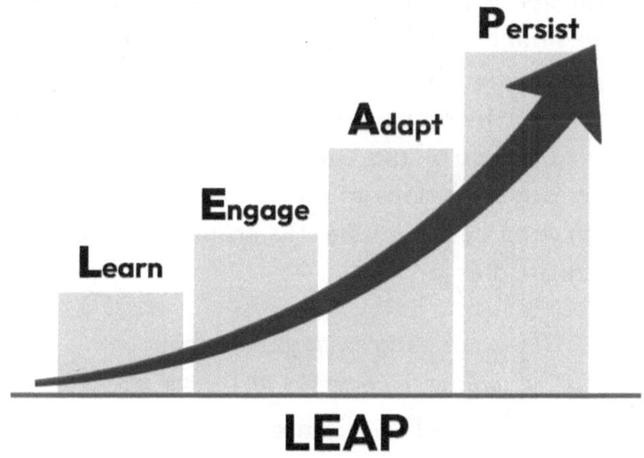

1. Learn – Learning is the foundation on which you build your dreams. When you learn more, you get new ideas and new ways of doing things. Learning is the first step of preparation that inspires and empowers you to do more and be more. Learn from books, courses, training, mentors, and everyone around you, and use these learnings to do more and better work. I always believe that everyone gets old with age but only a few grow with age. Who are the ones who grow with age? The ones who continue learning.

2. Engage – Engaging is more powerful than just doing. When you are engaged in something, you are not just doing it physically. But you are actively involved in doing it with all your focus and attention. Engaging is a very beautiful meditative way of doing things. You can understand the difference being doing and engaging when you watch children do something. Most people when they are doing something, they are thinking of something else. But when kids do something, they are totally into that one thing, with their heart and soul. That is what I call engaging.

The quality of your work will dramatically increase and so will your fulfilment when you are fully engaged in doing one thing at a time with full focus. When you are engaged hundred per cent in your work, you will be able to harness the unlimited power of the Universe and surprise yourself with new creative solutions to challenges that you felt you could not solve earlier. So master the art of engaging fully in whatever you are doing.

If you believe in what you are doing,
then let nothing can hold you up in your work.
– Dale Carnegie

3. Adapt – As you learn more and do more, you always get richer. As you do more, you will either get the results that you want, or you will get new insights which teach you a better way to get the results you want. So keep improving your action plans based on your learnings. When you adapt your learnings into your actions, you get success easier and faster.

4. Persist – Countless books have been written and millions of videos have been uploaded all over the internet about the power of persistence. Everyone knows it, but it is still very rare to find people with persistence. I urge you, my friend, when you already know that persistence is the key to success, why don't you step up today and decide to make persistence your superpower? You can never lose if you don't quit. Start taking actions, adapt to the feedback, take new actions and repeat. Persistence in the face of difficulties, setbacks, and criticism is a sure-shot way to unlimited achievements.

A word of caution on persistence. Why have I consciously chosen to write about persisting only after adapting? It is simply because if you continue doing the same things, you will continue getting the same old results. If you don't learn from your mistakes and just keep repeating those mistakes again and again in the name of persistence, how will you ever achieve your goals? You can complain your whole life about not getting what you wanted despite being persistent for so many years. But repeating activities that don't produce results will only make you a master of useless activities, nothing more.

You cannot open a lock by persistently putting the wrong key inside that lock. I don't call such people persistent; I call them stupid. Persistence without learning from mistakes and without finding smart solutions is pure stupidity. I believe life's winning formula is to be persistent in the pursuit of your dreams, but to be flexible and creative in your approach and working methodology.

So, make LEAP your secret weapon in every area of your life. I wish you a life and career where you keep Learning, Engaging, Adapting and Persisting.

An idiot with a plan can beat a genius without a plan.
– Warren Buffet

Have you heard about unfair advantage in the business? Unfair advantage is a distinct quality or trait that a person or company has that is tough to copy and that enables that person or company to be way ahead of other players in the same industry. I strongly believe preparation can be your unfair advantage because everyone wants to win, but very few people are committed to preparing for their victory.

You may sometimes feel that you may not have adequate talent, skills, education, language, background, inner circle or some other resources to win, but preparation is where all these excuses come to an end because you don't need any resources for preparation. If you are committed to preparing, you can achieve anything you desire. Why most people don't do it is because it needs a high level of commitment or seriousness to go through the process of preparation. Actually, your commitment to preparation is the test that proves how serious you are about your dreams.

You can achieve anything you want provided you are willing to pay the price for the same.

If you are really committed to achieving your dreams, here is the preparation framework that I and all my high-performance coaching clients have been using. This framework will empower you to do a comprehensive preparation before launching yourself into the pursuit of your dream. Your preparation will be complete when you prepare well in all five areas

1. Enhance your Capabilities
2. Build the Right Team
3. Align your Systems with your Goals
4. Money Management
5. Emotional Resilience

1. Enhance Your Capabilities

Every next level of success demands the next version of you. You cannot expect to scale new heights of success by working with the old level of mindset, skills and daily working habits.
– Deepak Bajaj

After training and working with more than two million people in the last twenty years, I have realized that not enhancing one's capability is the biggest reason why people stay stuck at the same old levels. While they blame their failure on multiple factors, they fail to realize that not upgrading their mindset, skills, and ways of working is the biggest bottleneck in their success.

As you set your eyes on your new big dream, clearly identify who you need to become to get the new results that you now dream of. Imagine the results that you are looking for and then imagine who is the kind of person that gets the results you want. What does that person do—how they think and handle people, how they communicate and manage finances and how they handle failures, setbacks and rejections?

Once you have a clear picture of who you need to become, you need to do what I call a MHS Gap Analysis, Mindset, Habits and Skills Gap Analysis, on any diary or notebook as per the format given below or using **Dream to Reality in 5 Steps – Journal & Workbook.**

MHS Gap Analysis

	What you need?	What you have?	What's the Gap?
Mindset			
Habits			
Skills			

In the first column, write down what kind of mindset, habits and skills you need to achieve your dreams. In the second column, write down what is your current level of mindset, habits, and skills. Now compare the two and clearly identify the gap in mindset, habits and skills that you need to bridge to become who you need to become and write the same in the third column. This one sheet of MHS Gap analysis has proven to be a total game-changer for lakhs of my trainees. I highly recommend you do it as early as possible, preferably today.

Every skill you acquire doubles your odds of success.
– Scott Adams

Once you have identified the new skills, mindset, or habits that you need to adopt, don't just stop there. Find out the best mentors, courses, training programmes, or free resources, and get on a mission to make yourself the best version of yourself. Remember the key is not just having goals or PDAs. The real game is to become the new person and once you have become this new version of yourself, new results will be automatically forthcoming.

When you start working on enhancing your capabilities, you need to work in two different areas

1. Refine and enhance your existing capabilities
2. Develop new capabilities that are required for new goals

For example, if you are a sales professional and you want to excel in selling, you need to develop skills like prospecting, conducting business meetings, objection handling and sales closing. Sharpening these skills will definitely help you become a better sales professional. But if your goal is to rise to the level of a sales manager or head of the sales department, then you will also need to develop leadership and managerial skills, so that you can motivate, train, mentor, and successfully lead a team of sales professionals to deliver the sales goals of the organization.

Why many great designers, teachers, doctors, or lawyers who are excellent in their field, cannot become successful entrepreneurs when they start their ventures in the same industry is because being an entrepreneur and head of a corporation requires many other capabilities than just designing, teaching, or doing medicine or law. This is the same reason why countless people in insurance or network marketing are not able to grow in spite of being great sales people because team management and leading people towards achievement of organizational goals is entirely different from doing something all by yourself.

When doing the skill gap analysis, please don't forget to study the high-success skills of your industry. In every industry, there are a few core principles and specific skills that contribute the most towards success in that particular industry. It is really important to identify those high-success skills and improve yourself on those skills. Also do remember to consider the current trends in your business. Every few years, new developments in technology, social media, AI and other socio-economic changes disrupt the way any particular business is done. If you can adapt to the trends, it will be easier to achieve big success.

Please remember if you do random things, you will get only random results. But if you do the right things at the right time with the right methodology, you will get specific results. Success is easier and faster when you become a master of high-success skills.

With more than two decades of experience in training and coaching people, I can tell you with absolute conviction that any dream can be achieved if people do MHS analysis immediately after setting their goals.

The future belongs to those who learn more skills and combine them in creative ways.
– Robert Greene

2. Build the Right Team

The bigger the dream, the more important the team.
– John C. Maxwell

One key determinant of whether you will be able to achieve your dream or not is your team. The scale of your achievements is directly proportional to the strength of your team. A good team not only multiplies the chances of success but also makes the journey enjoyable.

I was a good student in school and college. I was good at doing my homework, writing my exams, and anything that I had to do alone. But I was terrible at working in teams. I not only lacked confidence in communicating with people but also never believed that working together was better than working alone. As I set foot in the corporate world, I gradually realized that my sales performance was many times better in locations where we worked in teams that were aligned with each other, and worked with focus toward the achievement of team mission While I could observe the power of teamwork in multiplying sales volume, I could not replicate the same teamwork in all the places till I learned the nuances of building and nurturing the right team. As I started to master how to develop teams, I rose in my career to become one of the youngest regional managers in my company in 2005.

In 2007, I resigned from my job to pursue my first entrepreneurial venture. I broke all the records and became a top achiever in that business, again because of building and nurturing high-performance teams. Since 2018, I have been successfully running a training and coaching company and a few months back we started a branding, social media and digital marketing company as well. If I summarize, my key learning from the last twenty years of my career, it is this—you are only as strong as your team. You are only as big as your team. You are as smart as your team.

A dream without the right team and
systems is only a hallucination.
– Deepak Bajaj

Not just in the business world, but teamwork is at the core of every successful organization including a well-running home. Although it may appear that one person is running the show, success in every home, sports team, political party, corporation, social service organization or any other venture in life or business is invariably the result of teamwork. So, as you start working in the pursuit of your dream, please remember to build the right team. As the quality and work dynamics of your team improve, so will the height of your achievements.

There is no such thing as a self-made man.
You will reach your goals only with the help of others.
– George Shinn

Now the good news is if you have never been a good team player, don't worry. Being a team player is a skill that can be developed. While developing team skills, please remember, that we all have unique personalities, and while you can develop some key qualities and skills that can help you lead the team better, it is absolutely okay to have your own unique team management style. When you work on becoming a great team leader, you need to work on two different areas. Becoming an A player yourself and developing a team of A players. Let me quickly share some insights that can help you on your journey to be a team leader.

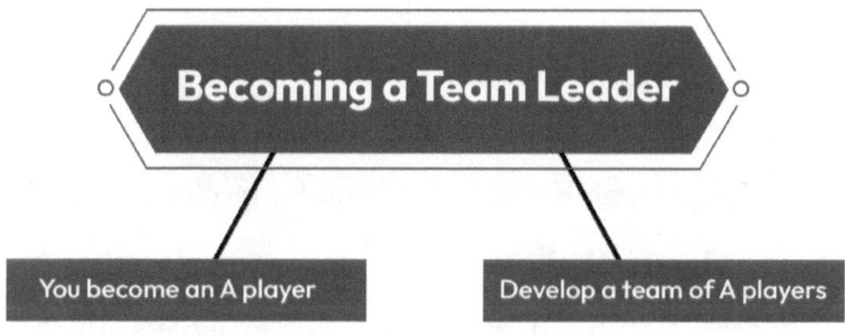

The first thing you need to do is to work on yourself to become an A player. The rule is simple. You don't attract what you dream, but you will attract only who you are. The speed of the engine is the speed of the train. If you really want to have A players in your team, you need to become an A player yourself because the best people will never work with an average leader. So learn more, do more and keep getting better at what you do. The domain of your expertise can be anything, but you should demonstrate the highest level of personal standards, working style, work ethics, values, and drive for excellence.

Great things in business are never done by one person;
they're done by a team of people.
– Steve Jobs

When it comes to developing a great team, I can offer you a very powerful formula that is easy to remember, simple to implement, and proven for its results. It has helped me and thousands of my high-performance coaching clients for two decades. I call it IDEA. Here is IDEA formula for Team Development

- **I**dentify right people
- **D**evelop them
- **E**nvironment to fuel their performance
- **A**ccountability of each person for results

1. Identify Right People

Identifying the right people is key to success. The best thing about the right people is that they need the least monitoring and they are able to take charge of the work faster. Whether you are in a corporate job, entrepreneurship venture, network marketing, or affiliate marketing, always be on the lookout for the right people and whenever you spot them, get them on the team.

2. Develop Your Teammates

The best of the diamonds also need polishing and so do all talented people. Don't leave people's development to chance. Make it a regular system in your organization or team to train and coach people. Give them the right opportunities to unleash their talent. Put people in different teams or projects so that they can learn from each other as well. Give them your time whenever possible and stand with them if they happen to make any mistakes. Make people development an organizational priority.

The strength of the team is each individual member.
The strength of each member is the team.
– Phil Jackson

3. An Environment That Fuels Their Performance

A money plant in a small vase on the table always stays small but the same money plant when planted in a garden can climb several floors. What has changed? The environment. Environment influences performance and has been proven in several studies to be a major determinant of people's performance. You must have seen that students' performance dramatically change when their school or college is changed. Many people who are not able to perform well in one company, start doing great in another organization. The same person will display different behaviour based on where he or she is—home, gym, temple, office, or discotheque. Environment has proven itself to be one of the biggest determinant to people's performance.

So your key job as a leader is to build an environment where A players love to be together, work together and perform at their best. Environment builds the culture and the culture attracts and retains the best talent. You need to build an environment that promotes a culture of trust, transparency, mutual support, growth, accountability, and excellence. Reward performers and deal assertively with the non-performers.

4. Accountability of Each Team Member

Accountability is a critical virtue I always look for in

team members. Accountability is total ownership of the work given. When you are accountable you do your work without reminders and you deliver on your promise. A person who is accountable does what he or she says and says what he or she does. Accountability builds trust and reputation. As you or your team grow in the leadership ranks, accountability stands higher than any other quality.

So build a great team using the IDEA formula and continue rising in your leadership.

Coming together is a beginning. Keeping together is progress. Working together is a success.
– Henry Ford

IDEA Formula for developing Great Teams
Identify right people
Develop your teammates
Environment to fuel their performance
Accountability of each person for results

3. Align Your Systems with Your Goals

A good system shortens the road to the goal.
– Orison Swett Marden

The biggest challenge after developing a good team is to keep that team actively engaged in meaningful activities that automatically deliver the desired results. You cannot be with each and every team member all the time. Team members will face different situations. Each of the team members will go through different moods and emotions every day. People may forget a few things, or may not like to do certain things. It is practically not possible to organize training and motivation sessions every week. Every team member has different capabilities and approaches to handing different people and situations. In this scenario, how do you ensure people consistently do the right things so that the organization delivers the right results? The answer is systems.

A system is a set of activities, guidelines, techniques and tools that everyone in the organization needs to follow. Systems ensures that everyone does the right thing consistently and I strongly believe when the right things are done consistently results take care of themselves. Systems ensure that existing team members stay on track and that the new ones quickly get on track. Systems bring the clarity on how to handle concerns and grievances. System guide people when they are confused about what to do in certain situations.

First, you make the systems and then the systems make your organization.
– Deepak Bajaj

So whatever the nature of your work or organization and irrespective of the size of your dreams, if you want to scale up, establishing the right systems is the only solution. Some of you may say that you have tried a lot to set up systems but people don't follow it. Let me solve this puzzle for you with my two decades of experience in building systems for lakhs of individuals and organizations.

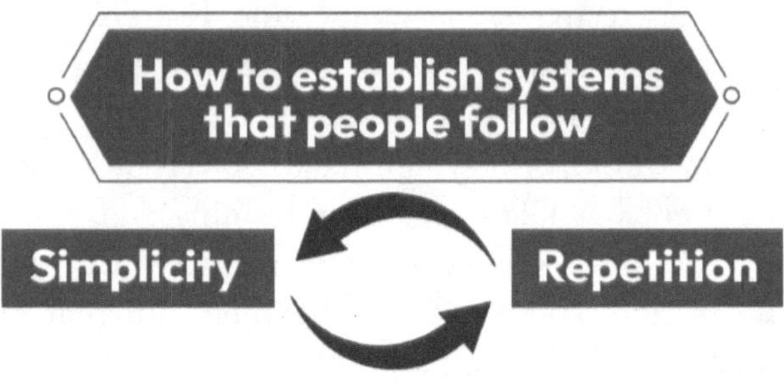

Two things that can help you establish systems:

1. Simplicity

It is human nature to avoid complex or difficult things. Given a choice, all of us would love to choose the path of least resistance. After training and coaching millions of people, I have deeply realized that people change when change is the only option. And the last thing you want to do is to follow the difficult paths. So the more complex the system, the greater the resistance in people to follow it. The simpler it is, the easier it will be to follow. So begin by designing a set of simple result-delivering tools and activities. When people get results by doing things in a certain way, they tend to follow more of that way. At the same time, don't be surprised and disheartened if some people don't follow the system. This happens in every organization. If these people are coachable and need a little extra hand-holding, please try that. If it doesn't work, find other people.

2. Repetition

My coach instilled very clearly in my mind that repetition is the mother of all success. So if you want your team to follow something, keep repeating it. Repeat it in your words as well as in your actions. Everyone will start following eventually, the only difference is for some people that eventually is today, and for some others, it might be after observing you for a few months. Whatever the case, keep repeating the good practices and people will eventually follow.

Many of my trainees ask me: how long should we repeat doing the right things so that everyone starts following? My answer is—forever. If you strongly believe that whatever you are doing is the right thing to do, why should you stop it? You continue doing it. If it is simple and produces results, eventually everyone will follow and as I said earlier, if some people don't follow, then follow this rule that I had written in detail in my fourth book :

If people don't change, change the people.

By the way, have you ever wondered, why repetition is so tough? Actually, repetition means doing the same things over and over again and doing the same things repeatedly is boring. When you start doing the same things day after day, month after month, year after year, you just get bored and you get tempted to try something new and fancy. When you are in a looking zone, something new will catch your attention and you will quickly go off track.

This is one of the biggest hazards of social media and internet. Every day, you will come across so many advertisements claiming that they can help you lose weight, build habits, earn millions, set up passive income, get financial freedom, or get you millions of followers, in just a few weeks. You were bored, and now here is a chance to stop doing whatever you were doing and start trying this new fancy formula. You forget to even check if all these tall claims have authentic validation of actually delivering the same results.

But this tendency to try every new fancy technique puts us off track. I am not asking you to stop trying new things or experiment with new ways of working. Do that once in three months or six months. But once you have found something that seems to work for you, at least repeat it consistently for a few months. Martial arts legend Bruce Lee put it beautifully–

I fear not the man who has practised 10,000 kicks once,
but I fear the man who has practised one kick 10,000 times.

Sometimes people stop doing the right things, over a period of time, because they look for shortcuts. Personally, I have seen that a lot of people are so obsessed about the results that, they feel that the entire journey of doing the spadework is like a punishment to them. I was also like that, madly, deeply obsessed only about getting the results anyhow, somehow. But I have realized that the magic happens when you fall in love with the process. Set the dream, identify what you need to do to get there and then joyfully do it every day with absolute trust in the process. Celebrate the journey.

4. Money Management

Earning a lot of money is not the key to prosperity.
How you handle it is.
– Dave Ramsey

Money is one of the most important factors in life and has been one of the hottest topics of discussion ever since it was invented. One key reason why I chose to include this subject here is that I have personally seen countless people, whose life and career have been ruined because of mismanagement of finances. There are two sides to money that you need to learn to master; one is about handling your current income, expenses, and lifestyle situation, and the second one is about managing finances for the future. Money management and investing is a big science in itself that needs more time and experience to master than just knowledge from books. Till you become an expert at money management, here are some of my recommendations that I have been personally following for many years

1. **Never buy what you don't need.** There are things you buy because you need them and there are plenty of others that you buy just because you feel having those things will make you more lovable, likable, influential, etc. or will upgrade your status. Please remember status is buying what you don't need with the money that you don't have to impress those who don't really care for you. So think twice before buying luxuries that you don't need.
2. **Never spend before you earn.** The first mistake is buying things that you don't really need and the second one is buying them on loan. Taking credit card loans or personal loans for luxuries or for showing off is the biggest financial disaster that can jeopardise your life and career.
3. **Manage loans carefully.** I am not talking about business loans here, but I am talking about all other loans including car, holiday, home, marriage, or any

other personal loan. Loans look tempting and easily manageable but if not handled properly, they can take away your freedom and peace of mind. A loan means committing a reasonable portion of your future earnings for today's expenses. Tomorrow will bring along many more expenses that you cannot foresee today. So think not twice but thrice before you take a loan for that new fancy phone, vacation, car or even a house.

4. **Saving is essential.** Make it part of your personality itself. One of the richest investors in the world Warren Buffet has repeatedly advised, '*Do not save what is left after spending, but spend what is left after saving.*'
5. **Build your Fund for the future.** Whatever you save, invest it judiciously. If you don't know where to invest and how to invest, learn it. No excuses, my friend. If money is important, then you better learn how to invest it so that it grows. Your future fund can be used for several things; entrepreneurship, early retirement, taking a break from work, or for some unforeseen contingencies. Having an adequate future fund will definitely give you a lot of peace of mind.
6. **Handle inter-personal loans carefully.** One reason for the end of many good friendships or relationships is loans between friends. Don't take a loan from friends and relatives. If you are forced to take one, return it before the committed time and as you had promised. Think twice before lending money to a friend as you may lose both the money as well as the friend.

7. **Never get into a situation when you don't have money to meet your basic needs** like rent, food, kid's school fees, etc. Continue building your contingency fund. Ask yourself how many days can you survive if your current income sources stop. Gradually build a six to twenty-four months contingency fund.

   Most people when they face such a financial crunch tend to make wrong decisions that worsen their already bad financial situation. Also, these are the moments when people tend to compromise their ethics and values and tend to do things which they regret later. To manage your expenses, save every month and invest those savings to build a future fund for yourself.

He who buys what he does not need steals from himself.

– Swedish Proverb

8. **Before you start taking action on any new project to fulfil your dream, understand the financial requirements for the completion of that dream.** Take help from some experts if you need it, but clearly identify the amount of money required to successfully complete the journey towards your dream. If you don't have enough money, explore means of arranging the required money so that you don't have to quit midway for the lack of money. Also, calculate the financial risk associated with your decisions and actions. It has been seen that lack of adequate finances or mismanagement of finances is one of the major reasons why many business ventures fail within the first few years of starting.

> While making a financial assessment, please remember that expenses tend to go beyond the original plan and income flow tends to be lower and slower than planned. So, make a contingency plan so that you don't have to abandon your dreams in case of an unforeseen situation. When I ask you to make a detailed financial plan, I want you to remember that risks are an inherent part of life and business. Risks are everywhere. Not doing anything is also a risk. My intention is to make you aware of the financial risks involved so that you are better prepared to handle the situations as they come.

So prepare yourself well, so that you control your money before it starts controlling your life.

A man who does not plan long ahead will find trouble right at his door.

– Confucius

5. Emotional Resilience

Don't allow your emotions to distract you from doing your work, instead do your work and distract your emotions.

– Deepak Bajaj

A good life and a career are invariably the result of your decisions and actions. Both of them are controlled by your moods and emotions. Many times in your life, you buy something and later wonder why you decided to buy that useless item. Many times you say something or do something, but later you wonder what made you say or do that. You make many big or small decisions in life about which you later feel surprised. You wonder what made you make those decisions. Actually, all those decisions and actions are taken in an emotional state which was not appropriate for taking that decision or action. I strongly believe if you can manage your emotions better it will dramatically elevate the quality of your decisions and actions and that would translate into better results.

I have been seeing countless people who know what to do, who have the talent, potential, degrees, and all the resources, who realize that it is important for them to do it, but still will not be able to take action. These are the people who have allowed their emotions to dictate their actions. Those who lose control of emotions will eventually lose control over their life and careers. Emotions are neither good nor bad. Emotions are just a state of mind or heart and we as social beings are bound to experience different emotions every day. There is nothing wrong with feeling sad, stressed or frustrated sometimes, but the problem begins when we allow it to interfere with our decisions and actions.

It is your reaction to adversity, not adversity itself that determines how your life's story will develop.
– Dieter F. Uchtdorf

Emotional resilience is your ability to maintain your calm in the middle of all crises and adversities. It is your ability to not allow outside events, people or their opinions to adversely affect your decisions and actions. You are emotionally resilient if you are able to continue doing whatever is right, whenever it is right, irrespective of whatever you are facing inside and outside of you.

Emotional resilience is a skill that can be developed. As you grow in your career, along with all your technical and leadership skills, emotional resilience will also play a role in determining the quality of your life and the trajectory of your career.

Here are a few insights to empower you to be more emotionally resilient

1. Take a decision right now to dissociate your actions from your mood, results or motivation. Countless men and women are paralyzed into inaction just waiting for the right mood or motivation to get started. Many others are gripped in the fear of failure or rejection, and continue preparing for months before they can actually start working. You know what you want and what you need to do to get there. Then, why have you allowed the mood or motivation to come in the way? Where is mood or motivation written in your action plan? If you did not give them any place on the paper where you made your plans, why are you giving them space in your mind and in your life? Just throw them away. They don't belong here. Take a decision right now to start taking action without even thinking about what mood you are in, or whether you feel motivated. Never worry about results. If you stay long enough with the process, results will take care of themselves. Keep working and keep adjusting your actions based on the results you are getting.

Two decades of professional career have taught me not to wait for the right mood or motivation to start taking action. Instead, you start doing the work and within minutes your mood and motivation will be uplifted. Try it for yourself.

2. Failure is a feedback. Failure is just an indicator that the current strategy and actions are not giving the results you expect. If you want different results, work with a different strategy and change what you are doing. Actions and Results are an iterative combination. Keep modifying till you get what you expect. In many cases, I have personally realized that even the goals I had initially set were not right. So, I have even redefined the results I was seeking. So just get going and keep improving with every feedback that failure gives you.

Courage isn't having the strength to go on,
it is going on when you don't have the strength.
– Napoleon Bonaparte

3. Always remember that your ability to handle stress, pressure, rejections, setbacks or bigger goals is like bicep muscles and you need to develop these exactly the same way you develop biceps or any other muscles. How do you build your biceps? You lift more weight than you are currently capable of lifting and you do it repeatedly. As you continue lifting more and more weight, your muscles start building. It is also called resistance training. You adapt your diet also to aid the process of building muscles.

In the same way, you build your emotional muscles when you take up more stress, pressure, or bigger goals than what you are currently used to handling. As you do it, gradually your capacity to handle more stress will also expand. You aid this emotional muscle-building process with a diet of new knowledge, training, coaching, and an empowering inner circle. As you continue this process, your emotional resilience will continue to expand. But it is as simple and as difficult as building your muscles. Everyone knows how to do it, but very rare people actually do it. That is why you find only a rare few people with great biceps and great emotional resilience. Happy emotional muscle building.

4. Difficulties are a reminder that you need to learn something new. If you feel something is difficult, it is not because of that particular work or goal. It is just because, right now, you don't know how to do it. The moment you learn how to do it, it will again become easy like everything else that you can easily do currently. At some point, writing A, B, C, and D was tough for you, speaking was tough for you, cycling or driving was also tough, and even reading this kind of book that you have in hand was tough for you. Everything that you are doing so effortlessly today was difficult at one point in time. But you learned it. Whatever seems difficult today, if you continue doing it, one day you will master it.

All my three kids are great basketball players. The ball just dances in their hands. They seem to just effortlessly move around the court and score point after point. But I cannot even dribble the ball for a few seconds. So playing basketball is easy or tough? It is easy for my kids but difficult for me. At the same time, you put me in a stadium with 10,000 people and I will keep them glued without moving out for many hours. During the Train the Trainer or advanced leadership workshops, I train people for five or seven days in a row. However, my kids find it difficult to speak for even three minutes in front of their class during their daily assembly. Speaking effectively in front of people is easy or difficult? It is easy for me, but difficult for my kids. So always remember nothing is easy or difficult forever. We make something easy or difficult with our attitude and approach towards it. If you really want to do something and are committed to learning it and practising it long enough, everything will be easy for you. Just go for it.

When we long for life without difficulties, remind us that oaks grow strong in contrary winds and diamonds are made under pressure.

– Peter Marshall

5. Anytime you catch yourself worrying about something, remind yourself to ask this question. Is it in my control? Just ask yourself, whatever you are worrying about right now. Is it in your control or not? If you are worrying about something that is not in your control, what is the point of worrying? If you are worrying about something that you can do something about, then why are you wasting time worrying instead of standing up and taking action?

Make mistakes, take decisions, do the best you can and when things don't work out the way you wanted, learn your lessons and ask yourself, '*What is the best thing I can do right now in this situation*' and do that.

6. Avoid the EBC virus. This one virus has killed more dreams than anything else in the world. I want you to be aware of this and avoid this at all costs.

EBC = Excuses, Blames and Complaint.

When you are making excuses, blaming or complaining, what you are actually doing is escaping from your responsibility for your current situation. When you are not responsible for something, how can you fix it? You can continue complaining and blaming for the rest of your life and it will not change anything. But if you take responsibility for whatever you have got, and whatever you have done, you can restart.

Also, I have personally seen that complaining and blaming negatively affect your mindset, emotions, and body. It breeds a victim mentality and puts you on a negative spiral of misery, sadness, and failure. Stay away from EBC and advise everyone also to stay away from this disease. If you want more knowledge on building your emotional resilience, you can visit my YouTube channel and Instagram account for several videos and other free resources.

7. Expect plans to fail. Plans are made to organize resources and to assign responsibilities so that action can begin. When you start actions, you get to see the situation differently, and you will unveil the smarter way to move forward. So be flexible after you have made the plan. When you start the action and you don't get the results you expected, it is not the time to quit. It is time to change what you have been doing.

Always remember there can be multiple ways of achieving your goal. Be firm about your goal, but be flexible about your approach. Find the best alternatives and keep moving ahead. Google Maps or the GPS apps on your mobile phone also work the same way. Anytime it finds a better route it gives you an alert that a faster route is available that can save five minutes and the app asks you to choose. What do you do in such a situation? You evaluate the options and choose the best route to your destination. It should be the same your everyday life. Keep your eyes and ears open as you work towards your goals and anytime you find a better route, opt for that.

Anytime you feel that a plan is not working out, smile broadly, pat your back and tell yourself that the time to work has come. Anybody can lead and take credit for everything that is going right, but what takes courage and indicates real leadership is how you handle the situation when things are not working out. Become a master of bounce back.

Do not judge me by my success, judge me by
how many times I fell down and got back up again.
– Nelson Mandela

A lot of insights and tools have been provided throughout this book that will empower you to handle different situations. Try out everything in it, and all the tools that you find from other sources. The key is to experiment with different tools and ideas to find out what works best for you. If you also have some other insights and ideas, do share them with me through my social media accounts or website, and we will incorporate the same in future editions of this book, on my videos or in one of my other future projects. Your inputs are priceless. I really appreciate them.

Preparation is your biggest ally to achieve your goals. When you are better prepared not only will you get good results in your current work but also more opportunities in the future. Preparation is an ongoing process. As you set new bigger goals, you will need new bigger preparation. Every cycle of setting goals, preparing for them, taking action and achieving them will make you a bigger and better person who will restart the cycle again with new higher goals and prepare for the same.

Setting a goal is not the main thing. It is deciding how you will go about achieving it and staying with that plan.

– Tom Landry

Warning – Although I have emphasised a lot on preparation as an essential element for success, I want to warn you against not using preparation as an excuse to delay taking action. There comes a point when you need to switch from preparing to acting and it is really important to be aware of that particular point, and jump to action once you have reached that point. Even though you may feel that you are not fully ready, trust me, many times the game is to begin before you are ready.

Right preparation definitively increases the odds of your success, and can save you from many mistakes that will cost you a lot of wasted time or money. Preparation is absolutely essential, but always remember that preparation is not equal to real work. Preparation is wonderful only if it is followed by timely, and determined action. Since preparation tends to expand itself according to the time available, it is always advisable to keep a deadline for the launch.

Decide the day and time when you will take off with the action and then force yourself to finish the preparation within the time available. Start with as much preparation as you can and continue the rest of the preparation as you go along. Anyway, preparation is a never-ending process and you will continue learning, doing, and growing throughout your life.

Start before you're ready. Good things happen when we start before we're ready.

– Steven Pressfield

As you start this beautiful journey towards your dream while preparing and working together on the go, you need to be aware of two zones of operations as shown in the diagram below

The preparation zone is the time when you become a student of your field and get obsessed about learning new things as if you know nothing. Performance zone is the time when you are at work and at that time you give your best performance with this deep underlying belief that nobody does this work better than you. You feel you are well prepared for the job and you play as if you are the best person on this earth to do this particular job. You should be aware of your zone, and then act according to the zone you are operating from.

When you are preparing, don't let your past knowledge and achievements come in the way of learning. I have seen thousands of good people in my workshops who fail to get the full transformation in the workshop because they are not able to forget their past achievements. While there are many others who go for their meetings constantly thinking about how much more they could have prepared before coming for the meeting, or how they could have carried that brochure or video and whatnot. They are doing the meeting, but they are constantly worried about the lack of preparation in their mind. Such people never get good results and fulfilment from the meeting. The key is to be wherever you are mindfully and work according to your zone.

So, if you are in the profession of sales, prepare as much as you want before the meeting, but once you are in the meeting with the client, work as if you are the best person in this field. Before going on stage with your speech, you can revise your notes and do as many rehearsals as you want. But as you step on to the stage, immediately switch from the preparation zone to the performance zone and own the stage as if you were born for it. You should deliver your speech with such great confidence that it has a tremendous impact on the audience – an impact that they will never forget.

If you play any sports, practice all your moves as much as you want before stepping on the ground but once you are on the ground believe, talk, walk and perform as if you are a GOAT of this game. (GOAT = Greatest of All Times). If you can master this mental switching from the Preparation Zone to the Performance Zone and vice versa, you will actually be on your way to being the best in your field.

You've got to jump off cliffs and build your wings on the way down.

– Ray Bradbury

Now, you know in depth about dreams, faith, and preparation. It is time now to take massive action and convert your dreams into reality.

Key Lessons from Chapter 3 That You Should Never Forget

- You can achieve anything you want provided you are willing to pay the price for the same. The price is preparation.
- Your confidence will go up and your fears and doubts will go down as you increase the level of your preparation.
- LEAP formula is a reminder of four key activities that you should continue to do as you pursue your dream. LEAP = Learn, Engage, Adapt, Persist.
- You cannot open a lock by persistently using the wrong key. Persistence without learning from mistakes or without finding smart solutions is pure stupidity.
- Five Areas of Effective Preparation – Capabilities, Systems, Team, Money and Emotions.
- Clearly identify who you need to become to get the new results that you dream of. Imagine the kind of person who gets the results you want, and you will start working to become that person.
- The scale of your achievements is directly proportional to the strength of your team.
- **IDEA** Formula for Team Development = Identify, Develop, Environment and Accountability.
- Scale, stability and consistency are the results of the right systems. Systems can be established by simplicity and repetition.
- Take a decision right now to dissociate your actions from your mood, results, and motivation.
- Avoid the EBC virus – Excuses, Blames and Complaints – at all costs.
- Always remember the two zones of operation – the Preparation Zone and the Performance Zone. Be conscious of your current zone and act accordingly.

Exercises to Strengthen Your Learnings from Chapter 3

1. Do your MHS Analysis today as per the format given in this chapter.
2. Evaluate yourself on all the four key aspects of LEAP – Learn, Engage, Adapt, and Persist. Give yourself a score on each of these parameters on a scale of zero to ten, with zero being the lowest and ten being the highest. You should do your LEAP analysis every month.
3. Evaluate yourself on five areas of Effective Preparation – Capabilities, Systems, Team, Money and Emotions. Identify the area which is weakest for you and make a plan to improve yourself in that area.
4. Evaluate the strength of your current team today. Identify the team you need to accomplish your dream and then compare it with the team that you have. Identify the gaps and make an action plan to build your dream team.
5. Scan the environment and systems at your place of work, and clearly identify the gaps. Make an action plan to build high-performance systems and environments.

Detailed forms to complete these exercises are available in **Dream to Reality in 5 Steps – Journal & Workbook.**
You can get this from my website www.deepakbajaj.biz or by scanning the QR Code alongside.

4

Massive Action

Dreams are useless unless they are supported by relevant daily actions and actions will never give you results and fulfilment if they are not aligned with your dreams.
– Deepak Bajaj

I have grown up hearing this key life philosophy often repeated in my family. A small action is better than a thousand noble intentions. Noblest of the intentions and best of the plans will only gather dust, if you don't take action on them. You will meet a countless number of men and women who can talk endlessly about dreams, life, businesses, wealth and every topic on earth. But their lives never change because they never do anything. Jim Rohn put it beautifully when he said, '*If you don't like where you are, move. You are not a tree.*' Action is the bridge between your current situation and your dream destination.

You know your dreams. You have absolute faith that you will get it. You have done the preparation. Now get to action without wasting any single minute. Why are people not able to take action after setting their dreams? One key reason is that people are very good at long-term planning and setting their two to five-year goals. But they just leave it to their willpower and judgement to take the necessary actions the next day. People don't complete the goal-setting process by fixing the exact details of what they need to do every day to achieve that goal.

Dreams don't work unless you do.
– John C. Maxwell

Training on goal setting is considered complete by making people write what they want to achieve in life. People write about cars, homes, bank balances, foreign trips, family holidays, recognition, impacting the world, social service, etc. You might have also attended several training programmes and would have written your dreams as I asked you to write in Chapter One of this book. Then, the trainers explain things like setting SMART Goals (Specific, Measurable, Action-oriented, Realistic and Time Bound), picturizing your dreams, and crystalizing them in your mind.

All these concepts are great. I had also tried them for many years. But the fact remains that if pasting photos of a car and taking a test ride were enough to get your dream car, every person would have been driving their dream car by now. Writing your dreams is a proof that you really want to grow in life. But, don't forget that writing them is merely a statement of intention. Writing goals and pasting pictures of them all around is the first step, and you need to walk the other four steps as well. If you seriously want to achieve your goals, please understand the distinction between two different kinds of goals.

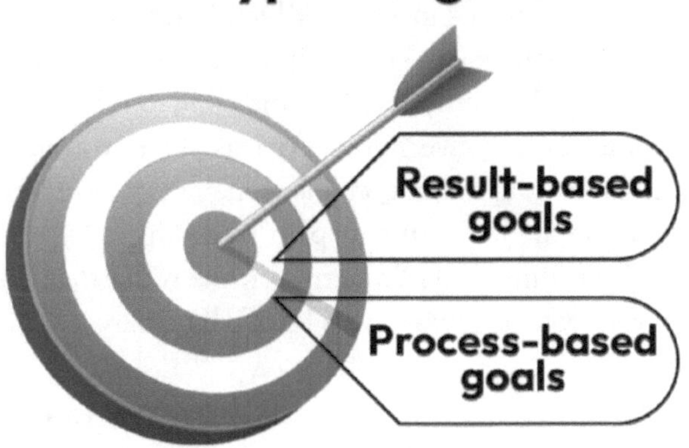

Your cars, house, rank, bank balance, etc. are all result-based goals. But, you cannot achieve your result-based goals till you set your process-based goals as well. Process-based goals are simply the daily actions that you need to perform to achieve your result-based goals. You need to be clear about which car you want to drive, but at the same time, you need to be very clear about what actions you need to take every day to achieve that car. Those actions become your process-based goals. Hence, clearly determining your daily and weekly actions is the most important step in preparing for the achievement of your dreams.

A real decision is measured by the fact that you have taken a new action. If there is no action, you haven't truly decided.

– Tony Robbins

Let me help you understand this point better with the example of how exactly the GPS/Google Maps app works on our phones. Take for example, you are in Delhi and you want to go to a nearby city, say Jaipur. The GPS app begins by asking you two things, your current location and your destination. In this case, your current location is Delhi and your destination is Jaipur. As soon as you enter Jaipur in your GPS app, it will immediately tell you the distance and time to reach Jaipur e.g. 300 kilometres and five hours. At this stage, you are seeing two things on your mobile app screen, 'Jaipur, 300 km and 5 hours.' If you are ok with this plan of reaching Jaipur in five hours by travelling 300 kilometres on the route that GPS has offered you, you can press the START button.

Now, as you press the START button, something interesting happens. Immediately, 'Jaipur, 300 km and 5 hours' will disappear and your GPS app will start showing you the next few meters and the next turn. For example, it may ask you to go straight for the next 500 meters and take a left turn. After that, it may ask you to continue for one km and take a right turn. As you keep moving ahead, GPS will tell you only about the next few meters or kilometres that you need to travel. Your dream destination is still Jaipur but all your attention and energy are directed towards effectively completing the next few meters. Your goal is to reach Jaipur but you start making progress only by travelling the next few meters at a time.

After experimenting with multiple approaches for accomplishing dreams, I have realized that when you approach any of our dreams, the GPS methodology seems to work the best. Decide your dream, make a daily action plan and then just forget about your dream and focus all your efforts on effectively doing the next step. As you are about to complete one step, you will see the next one and by effectively completing one step after the other, you will undoubtedly accomplish your dream.

Let me share with you a simple but very effective process of identifying the right daily actions to achieve your specific dream.

As soon as you set your eyes on a dream, immediately make a list of actions that you need to do every day to achieve your dream. Make as big a list as you want and write every small or big action that you think should be done on a daily basis to achieve that big dream. While you are making this list, be conscious about writing only those actions that are totally in your control. Write down only those actions for which you are not dependent on any other person or situation.

You may write as many actions as you want, but please be clear that all actions are not equally important when it comes to delivering the specific results that you want and it is also not possible to do all those actions every day. So, the key is to scan your list carefully and identify those three actions that you think will give you the best results. Be committed to completing those three actions every day before anything else. We call these three actions your PDAs, Primary Daily Actions.

After you have written your three PDAs, ask yourself this question, '*If I do these three PDAs every day for the next few months or years, will I achieve the most important dream of my life?*'

If your answer to this question is an absolute yes, please forget about your dream and start doing your PDAs every day. If your answer is no or a doubtful yes, please go back to your PDAs and make the necessary adjustments. Your goal is to identify three such specific PDAs about which you are 100 per cent confident that doing them will lead you towards the accomplishment of your dreams.

The key objective of this exercise is to simplify your life and empower you to make daily consistent progress in the direction of your dreams. After you have identified your PDAs, you should not think about your big dream. Rather you should focus all your energy on completing your PDAs as effectively as you can. This shift in the focus from big dreams to daily PDAs can help you achieve any of your dreams, be it writing a book, or losing weight, or achieving a certain rank, or buying your dream car. I have personally achieved all my life goals through this process and so have lakhs of my workshop trainees. Gaining this clarity about the next step can be your biggest game-changer and the PDA process helps to do it for you.

A word of caution. While determining your PDAs, please decide actions that you can complete in a day. In your overenthusiasm to achieve your big dreams faster, don't decide on actions that you will not be able to do every day on a consistent basis. Please remember the goal is daily consistent progress. Once you have built the consistency, you can increase the intensity of your actions.

I call this entire model Life GPS System. When used properly, it can empower anyone to achieve any goal and that too without any stress. This model has been illustrated in the diagram below

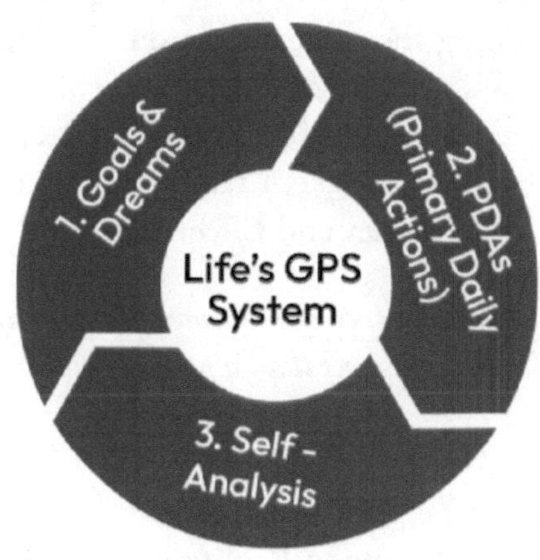

There are three components in this GPS system. You begin by setting your goals and dreams. Then you identify your PDAs and start doing your PDAs every day. After you have done your PDAs for thirty to forty-five days, you should review the progress you have made and make necessary adjustments to your PDAs. This is where a lot of people make mistakes. Whenever you start doing any new activities, after a few days of doing them, you tend to develop a sense of comfort in doing some of the activities. You just continue doing them month after month without analysing the results they are producing. But if you are really serious about making progress, you need to make a system for monthly and quarterly self-analysis and follow this simple rule. Do more of what is working and do less of what is not working. I have written more and proposed a model for self-analysis in the next chapter.

Some actions, which were really good for you, and gave you amazing results when you started them a few years back, may not be effective anymore. You should actually stop doing them and replace them with new actions that will give us new results. It is futile to complain about not getting new results by repeatedly doing the same old actions that have lost their relevance. Always remember that you become efficient by doing actions repeatedly and you become effective when you choose which actions to take. I really want you to be E^2 **= a combination of Efficiency and Effectiveness.**

Take action! An inch of movement will bring you closer to your goals than a mile of intention.
– Steve Maraboli

To help you take the right actions consistently, I have created a special **Dreams to Reality in 5 Steps – Journal & Workbook** that can be used with this book. This journal has detailed forms that you can just fill out and complete all the steps that are described in this book. You can order a copy of that workbook from my website www.deepakbajaj.biz.

Have you seen people who are experts at setting big goals but are not able to take action due to a lack of motivation? Or some others who set such big goals that they are crushed under the weight of their own goals. There are many other ambitious people with big motivation who make such long To-do lists that just by looking at the size of their lists they are paralyzed to inaction. My PDA system addresses all these concerns and will empower you to make daily consistent progress towards your dreams.

There is another hidden benefit of completing your PDAs everyday. Every time you complete your PDAs, your confidence and self-belief will also be uplifted and you will give a message to your subconscious mind that you always do what you decide to do. Continuously achieving your goals will strengthen your subconscious beliefs and set you up for ever-growing success.

Everyone knows the power of the subconscious mind and what it can do for you. But the most important task is to programme your subconscious mind to work in your favour. The PDA method done rightly will programme your mind for big success. If you want to learn how to train your subconscious mind, you can watch a short video on my YouTube channel. It will answer many of your questions related to success and the subconscious mind, and also give you a simple approach to effectively train your subconscious mind. You can watch it by scanning the QR code below.

YouTube Video - How to train your subconscious mind?

Do not believe that you will reach your destination without leaving the shore.

– Chinese Proverb

Now, since you are absolutely clear about three things you need to do everyday to make your dreams a reality, just go for it. Be committed and disciplined to do everyday what you have decided. Every time you commit to other people, you do your best to honour that commitment. Why not do the same for the commitments you make to yourselves? If you have decided that you will do these three things every day, why sacrifice them for other people or other things? Whenever you do what you have planned, you strengthen the inner winner inside you and that is how you will gradually build the internal strength to aim for higher goals.

Commitment is doing something long after the mood to do what you have promised yourself to do, has gone. Self-discipline is doing the right things at the right time, irrespective of whether you feel like doing it or not. Make commitment and self-discipline your best allies and be on the fast track to achieving your dreams.

Be a person of action. Develop the reputation of someone who does what he or she says. Become a no-reminder person. If you have committed to do something, the world knows that you will do it without any reminders. As you develop these qualities, success and abundance will automatically find their way towards you.

When you start taking action, always be on guard for the seven biggest enemies that may stop you from taking action, as given in the diagram below:

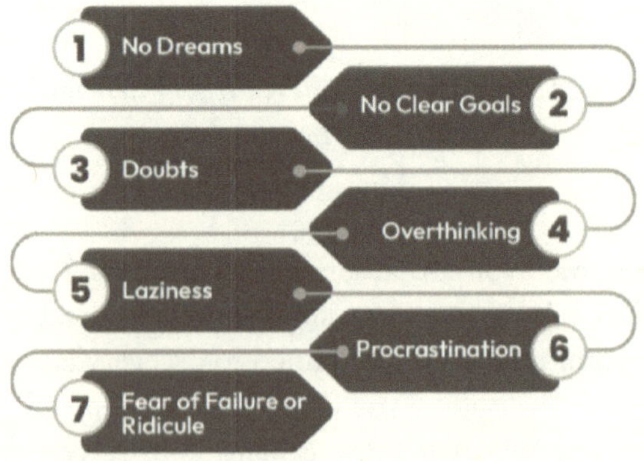

1. No Dreams or Drive – You will not stop at a restaurant, however amazing is their food, if you are not hungry. If you don't want to go anywhere why will you make any effort to go? People never take any action, if they lack dreams or purpose.

2. No Clear Goals – Working without clear goals is similar to driving a car with a dusty windscreen. The fastest of the cars also cannot take you forward, if you cannot see the road ahead. Likewise, if you don't know clearly where you want to go, how will you take the next step? Clarity precedes success.

3. Doubts – Doubts have killed more dreams than the lack of any other resource. How will others believe in you when you don't even believe in yourself? Don't listen to this voice in your head that tells you, '*What if it will not work out*?' Ask that voice to shut up and, trust me, this voice will actually shut up, if you assertively command this voice to shut up. Anytime you get this doubt '*What if it doesn't work out*?' change the narrative immediately and tell yourself, '*What if it actually works out as planned*?' and get going.

4. Overthinking – Some people keep waiting for that perfect time or moment, when they can say that everything is ready and that they can begin doing what they want to do. This approach is fine but the only problem is that there will never be a moment when you will be able to say that. Get out of this never-ending loop of getting ready. Yes, preparation is important. I have written a whole chapter on preparation in this book. But I want to warn you to put a time limit to your preparation and quickly move to the next stage of action.

You can use two of my proven formulas to instantly propel you to action

1. Start now and improve later
2. Eighty per cent is good enough

If you feel you are eighty per cent ready, just begin the action. Anyways, the first product is not the final product. Keep improving. Currently, the iPhone is selling its fifteenth version and the current model of Mercedes E Class is the sixth-generation model. Start now and keep improving later.

A dream doesn't become reality through magic;
it takes sweat, determination, and hard work.
– Colin Powell

5. Laziness – For various reasons, people are just lazy and not willing to take any action to change their life or work situation. You may wonder if these people don't want to earn more money. Well, the strategy for these people is to keep minimising their lifestyle and keep reducing their expenses so that they can manage with the lowest income. They love rest, recreation and staying wherever they are.

6. Procrastination – While laziness is not doing anything, procrastination is doing everything else but not doing the work that is absolutely important for your goals. They are people with good intentions and they know what to do, but they are so comfortable doing certain low-value activities that they keep making excuses to avoid doing the real work. They have mastered the art of appearing busy. They will just keep postponing their high-income tasks or growth activities in the name of doing something else.

Actually, most of the people, including me, procrastinate at some level or the other. The best way to beat procrastination is by following the GPS model as discussed earlier in this book, working with a mentor, or having an empowering inner circle. Going for new training also opens up your mind to doing new things. I have made several free training videos on how to beat laziness and procrastination. You can find them on my YouTube channel.

Get so busy improving yourself that you have no time left to think about what others are thinking or doing.
– Deepak Bajaj

7. Fear of Failure or Ridicule – Our parents wanted us to be good sons or daughters. Our school or college wanted us to be a good student. Society wanted us to be a good person. The definition of good that has been repeatedly drilled into us is someone who is disciplined, obedient, does not make mistakes, listens to their parents, teacher or relatives, does whatever is being told by seniors, and follows whatever everyone else is doing. If you don't fit into this definition, you will be labelled as a bad boy or girl. You will be scolded. Your parents or teachers will not like you and everyone around you will laugh at you.

Every time we made a mistake we were scolded and punished. Every time we questioned what everyone was doing or gave a different answer or used a different approach, everyone around us made fun of us. Society just wanted us not to be troublemakers, and quietly follow the norm. I am not getting into why and how such a system was introduced, but since our childhood, we have developed this fear of making mistakes and fear of being laughed at. Before we do anything new or even think about it, our first worry is, '*What will other people say*?'

Trust me, most of us overestimate how much we will be laughed at, or talked about by others for our failures. Most people don't care what you are doing or not doing unless you are a celebrity, or the most successful business owner or political leader of your city. And among all those people who talk about your failure, most people will even forget about your failures within minutes of it. Just like you, they are also busy worrying about their own failures. Also, remember that those people whom you are scared of will say something or the other even if you don't do anything. Have you noticed who are these people who always talk negatively about others? They are typically the ones who are big losers and failures themselves. They are the ones who never worked hard, and never did anything significant in their own life, and the only option they have to safeguard their cowardice is to pull every high dreamer down so that everyone stays at their level.

So never stop doing what you truly believe because of this worry about what people might say. Always remember this quote by Brené Brown, '*Courage is like – it's a habitus, a habit, a virtue: You get it by courageous acts. It's like you learn to swim by swimming. You learn courage by couraging.*'

I heard this story many years back about one father and son who went to buy a donkey from a village animal market. While they were coming back to the village with the donkey, they met some people who laughed at them saying, '*You both are the biggest idiots in this village, who have bought the donkey but still walking and not sitting on the donkey. Why did you buy the donkey if you don't sit on it?*' Both of them got upset by seeing people laugh at them and immediately climbed on the donkey's back. Now, they were very confident that people around them would be proud of them.

After some time, they came across another bunch of people, who became really angry seeing both the father and the son sitting on the donkey. They said, '*How can you be so cruel that both of you are sitting on the poor donkey? The donkey is almost dead because of carrying two adult men on its back. Have some pity.*' Both got really disturbed hearing this and got off the donkey's back. They got really confused about what to do because people laughed at them when they were not sitting on the donkey as well as when they were sitting on the donkey. The father came up with the plan that the son would sit on the donkey and the father would just walk along. They both were super confident that this time nobody would laugh at them as only the son was sitting on the donkey's back now.

After a while, they came across another bunch of people, who got really mad at them, saying, '*What an unfortunate sight. The young son is sitting on the donkey's back and the poor old father is walking in the sun. It is better not to have a son than having such a cruel son.*' The duo got really disturbed now and the only option they had now was to make the father sit on the donkey's back and let the son walk by the side. They were super confident that now people would appreciate them and be proud of them.

Again, they came across another bunch of people who again reprimanded the duo by saying, '*What a selfish father this fellow is, making his son walk in the sun and is riding the donkey himself. All his life, the father has enjoyed and now it is time for the son to savour life. But this cruel father is still so evil that he is riding the donkey himself and is not allowing the son to ride it.*'

The father and son had tried every possible option in the expectation that people would appreciate them. But whatever they did people just laughed at them. The only option left with them now was to carry the donkey on their shoulders. They wanted to please the whole village so much that finally they carried the donkey on their back and entered the village. They entered the village with big pride on their faces and confidence in their heart with the expectation that now the whole village would appreciate them. To their immense surprise, the entire village started laughing at them saying, '*This father and son are the biggest idiots we've ever seen in our lives. Why did these two buy the donkey in the first place if they have to carry it on their shoulders.*'

They both got so disheartened that they started crying, left the donkey, and ran to their home. Trust me, the saddest and the most miserable people on this earth are the ones who always try to please others. Please stop trying for this, you will never succeed. Instead, do something that you will be proud of. Do things that will help you achieve your goals and fulfil the dreams of your family.

A YouTuber with a million followers will never make fun of your first video however bad it is. A good trainer will never make fun of your first speech. A great entrepreneur will never ridicule you for starting a small side hustle. Never leave your track because of those who are not on track themselves.

You are the only person responsible for fulfilling the dreams of your family. I have personally experienced that none of these people who act as advisers will come to your rescue if your family goes through a tough situation. So why worry about what these people say about you? If you start thinking what they are thinking, then when will they do some thinking of their own? You do your thinking, let them do their thinking and always remember

Never stop working for your dream, worrying about the opinion of your neighbours because the opinion of your neighbours will instantly change after seeing your success.

– Deepak Bajaj

Decide right now to be an action-taker. Everyone is full of ideas and opinions. Social media and the internet have flooded everyone with all the knowledge and ideas. The world is full of experts, trainers and coaches but what really separates the winners from everyone else is the speed of execution. You may not be a first mover in your industry. That is ok. But you can definitely be the fast mover. Anyway, first-mover advantage is a thing of the past. Now, it is all about being the fast mover. Adopt this new philosophy from today – Let's do it now.

Think big, think fast and think ahead.
Ideas are no one's monopoly.
– Dhirubhai Ambani

Key Lessons from Chapter 4 That You Should Never Forget

- Many people consider their goal-setting process complete just by writing their goals or dreams. But you must go on to clearly identify your top three actions that you will do every day to achieve those goals. You will call these top three actions your PDAs (Primary Daily Actions).
- There are two types of goals—Result-based goals and Process-based goals.
- Become a master of the Life GPS System for fulfilling any Dream – Goals/Dreams>PDA (Primary Daily Actions)>Self-Analysis.
- You become efficient by doing actions repeatedly. But you become effective when you choose which actions to take. So, aspire to perform with a combination of efficiency and effectiveness.
- Make commitment and self-discipline your best allies to be on a fast-track to achieving your dreams.
- Always be on guard against the seven enemies of action; No dream, no clear goals, doubts, overthinking, laziness, procrastination and the fear of failure or ridicule.
- The saddest and the most miserable people on this earth are the ones who always try to please others. Please stop doing this, or you will never succeed.
- Never stop working for your dreams, and don't worrying about the opinions of others because their opinions will instantly change after seeing your success.
- Everyone has ideas. The world is full of experts, trainers and coaches. But what really separates the winners from everyone else is the speed of execution.
- When it comes to moving from preparation to action, always remember these two rules.
    1. Start now and improve later.
    2. Perfection is unattainable. Eighty per cent is good enough.

Exercises to Strengthen Your Learnings From Chapter 4

1. Follow the step-by-step PDA identification process as given in this chapter to identify your PDAs.
2. After identifying your PDAs ask yourself this question: "If I do these three PDAs every day for the next few months or years, will I achieve the most important dream of my life?" If your answer to this question is an absolute yes, please forget about your dream and start doing your PDAs every day.
3. Imagine yourself doing your PDAs and predict some of the possible obstacles that can stop you from doing this consistently. Find some quick solutions for the same right now, and start action on your PDAs.
4. Examine all seven enemies of action, and check if you have faced anyone or any of those in the past. Devise a strategy for handling the same when it occurs again in the future.

Detailed forms to complete these exercises are available in **Dream to Reality in 5 Steps – Journal & Workbook.**

You can get this from my website www.deepakbajaj.biz or by scanning the QR Code alongside.

5

Ecosystem for Success on Autopilot

If you have a dream, don't just sit there.
Gather the courage to believe that you can succeed
and leave no stone unturned to make it a reality.
– Roopleen

Our first goal in life is to be successful and then the second one is to maintain the success or to multiply our success. In the heart of the heart, everyone wants to grow and rise. We want to flourish in all different areas of life, and in all different dimensions of our career. We have multiple talents that we want to express and multiple things we want to do. While many people are not able to set goals and start actions, there is a big majority of those who have goals and desires. They are also motivated and start the action, but they are not able to do the right actions consistently and hence not able to create the life they dream of. In most of these cases, people miss out on creating the fifth element of success and that is creating the right environment.

If you are not able to maintain consistency in your actions and continuous growth in your performance, the first thing you need to check is your ecosystem. The right ecosystem will not only make success automatic for you, but also provide you with deep fulfilment on your success journey.

I believe your key objective in life is to design an ecosystem
for you in such a way that success becomes automatic,
continuous growth happens naturally and true
fulfilment becomes an integral part of your life.
– Deepak Bajaj

An ideal success ecosystem principally consists of daily rituals and review systems that ensure consistency and growth in all the nine key areas of life. Two decades of professional career, training and working with two million plus people and interacting with thousands of ultra-successful people in all walks of life have taught me that work is one part of life and not the whole life. When you are working to build your dream life, why not include good health, blossoming relationships and lasting happiness as part of our dream life?

I have written a very special bonus chapter in this book on nine key areas of good life. Once you complete this chapter on success ecosystem, please don't forget to read the next chapter on creating holistic success in all areas of life so that you not only create huge wealth but also enjoy your wealth everyday with good health, quality relationships, and ultimate fulfilment.

An ecosystem that can make success on autopilot for you has seven key components as illustrated in the diagram below:

Do the best you can until you know better.
Then when you know better, do better.
– Maya Angelou

1. Power Rituals

Rituals are simple actions that you do every day to get the life you want. The power of rituals lies in their simplicity and in their ability to empower you to evolve into the best version of you. Anything and everything important that needs to be done every day must be converted into simple daily rituals. Any action becomes a ritual when you specifically define these four things—what is to be done; when will it be done; where will you do it and how will you do it. It is not enough to say that you will read every day or even that you will read for fifteen minutes every night before sleep. I highly recommend you go one more step further and answer the four questions that I have specified above.

The same night reading activity will become a ritual when you say something like: I will read the book (----name of the book-----), for fifteen minutes while in my bed at 10.30 p.m. I recommend that you keep that book also on the side of your bed. Don't think that you will bring it from your almirah when you begin to read it. Keep it there right now, and let that book be there by your bedside till the time you complete reading it. You can even set an alarm in your phone that says DEAR, Drop Everything and Read, at 10.25 p.m.

Please don't tell me that you are so motivated that you will do it even without all this. I am not questioning your motivation or willpower, I just want to make sure that this time, whatever you decide must happen without fail, and I don't want to leave any stone unturned to ensure the same. I want you to seal all possible loopholes right now, right here. I am particular about it because of two main reasons

1. The way you do one thing is the way you do everything. If you can plan and execute small things like fifteen minutes of reading so well, imagine if you carry this same strategy and style to your bigger goals. You can easily accomplish them as well.
2. Deciding and succeeding are a habit and so does deciding and not doing. You become what you repeatedly do. If you don't do small things like fifteen minutes of reading well, how will you successfully complete bigger projects? From this very moment onwards, I really want you to be very particular about everything you think, decide and do because the goal is not that activity but the goal is to make you into a person who can achieve anything he or she wants.

Honouring the commitments that you make to yourself is one of the highest forms of self-love. It will uplift your self-image, confidence and of course your success.

– Deepak Bajaj

Always remember, whatever is important should never be left at the mercy of willpower or chance. Convert them to rituals and do them every day. You need to set rituals for each of the nine areas of your life and include them in your daily, weekly or monthly cycle of doing things. The Primary Daily Actions (PDAs) process that we discussed in Chapter Three is one of the best ways to identify your daily rituals.

One big mistake people make while setting their PDAs or Daily Rituals is to overestimate what they can do in a day. In the rush of excitement, they decide too big tasks to do every day but later, when they begin doing them, they cannot complete them. This feeling of failure, rejection and shame of not honouring their own commitment throws them off within a week or two of starting the action. And the beautiful transformation process that started with big hopes, ends there itself. Please remember to start with small actions. Build consistency, confidence and self-belief by doing those actions consistently and then continue scaling up.

Habit is a cable; we weave a thread of it each day,
and at last, we cannot break it.
– Horace Mann

You can set up rituals for three times of your day; morning rituals, day rituals and night rituals. You can decide your own specific rituals, but as a thumb rule here is what you should include in each of these sets of rituals

Morning Rituals – Gratitude, drinking water, healthy breakfast, workout, meditation, reviewing your top deliverables of the day, manifestations and prayers.

Day Rituals – Do your PDAs in your peak performance state, Day Review when you finish you work (write everything good that happened during the day, key learnings from today and top 3 deliverables for the next day) and some specific time slots during the day when you work on your most important projects with utmost focus and without any distractions

Night Rituals – Reading, journaling, gratitude, time with family, short meditation, avoiding food and social media at least two hours before sleeping. Doing something that you love before you end your day.

This is my recommended list. You are free to choose

whichever you want from this list and keep adding one new thing at a time.

Your rituals have the power to make or break your life. When you do your PDAs, the results may be unnoticeable in the first few days but a tiny one per cent progress everyday will add up to 365 per cent progress in one year and that will be big enough for the whole world to notice and totally change your game. Anyway, whatever you are doing currently throughout your day are also your rituals. But most of your current rituals are the ones that you have just adopted unconsciously without considering their future consequences. I want you to be aware of your rituals and consciously design your rituals and PDAs so that your dream life becomes a natural outcome of your daily working.

The difference between an amateur and a professional is in their habits. An amateur has amateur habits. A professional has professional habits. We can never free ourselves from habit. But we can replace bad habits with good ones.

– Steven Pressfield

Now since you have deeply understood the science of working with rituals, I invite you to look at PDAs and rituals from a different perspective. I want to share with you my personal experience with designing and doing my daily rituals that have elevated the quality of my life to an altogether new high. It is like living my dream life right now, right here. I invite you to have a new look at your PDAs with an open heart and mind.

Although most of us consider our rituals as the route to a happy and successful life, trust me, once you start loving life and start living a life with consciousness, these same rituals can become a daily celebration of a good life. Your route can become your destination. What if you looked at your PDAs not just as a vehicle to achieve your goals, but a goal itself?

Just imagine, how much you can elevate the quality of your life if you can find as much happiness in your daily actions as you find in the results. Why do you do PDAs or rituals? So that you can create the life you want. What if the very rituals become the life you really want? Why people cannot go to the gym every day because at some point going to the gym starts looking like a punishment. What if you start looking at going to the gym as a celebration of living a good life? You celebrate as you go through your grind and you know that the party will grow bigger as you continue going to the gym day after day.

Even after making one crore and driving a Porsche, you will be eating homemade food most of the time, will be doing some work in your office, will be doing workouts, meditations, gratitude, hobbies and spending quality time with your family. Why not include as many of these things as you can in your daily rituals right now in such a way that every day of your life can become a celebration right now and not sometime in the future? Trust me, as you start adding more and more of such activities in your daily life, you will start living your dream life right now right here. It is not very difficult if you start looking at your every day as an opportunity not only for preparing for life, but for living your life. Add some more gratitude, consciousness and right perspective to your life and you will claim your heaven right here, right now.

Sometimes the longest journey we make is sixteen inches from our heads to our hearts.

– Elena Avila

Let's do one exercise right now, which I call – **Creating My Own Heaven Today:**

Creating my own Heaven Today

1.	Make a list of what all you will include in your daily routine once you become super successful and achieve your dreams.
2.	What are some of the things on this list, that you can do right now?
3.	Can you start adding some of these things in your routine right now in whichever way you can? You can go on a long drive on a top model Harley Davidson bike when you will have one, but can you go on a long drive on whichever scooter you have right now? Why not begin with that? Drive is the same anyway.
4.	Now just close your eyes, put your hand on heart and take 11 deep breathes. Now imagine how you will feel when you see yourself doing some of these things everyday.
5.	Decide right now, which of these activities you are going to add in your daily routine from today.

I urge you to do this exercise right now. Please remember, you have twenty-four hours every day to work for your goals. Why can't you set aside just thirty minutes to an hour everyday to do what you love doing? Trust me, your goal achievement will not suffer due to these thirty minutes you've set aside. I strongly believe that these will add more passion, energy, life and productivity to the rest of your day. Give it a shot and do let me know your experience on my Instagram page or on support@deepakbajaj.biz.

The art of fulfilment is the ability to experience not only the thrill of the chase but also the magic of the moment, the unbridled joy of feeling truly alive.

– Tony Robbins

2. Space in your Home and Workplace

Your work desk, your dining table, your living area and other spaces around you can instantly indicate your priorities, level of success, health and overall quality of life. Space around you is one of the biggest determinants of whether you will be able to accomplish your daily PDAs or not. Your space will either make it easier for you to consistently practice your good habits, or it will make it a struggle. You cannot cultivate good habits without an empowering environment around you.

Start becoming conscious of how spaces around you are influencing your behaviour and once you start noticing the impact, start redesigning your environment so that the desirable behaviour becomes a habit for you.

Here are a few examples of small changes in your space that can reduce some of the struggles you face in building up good habits

- If you are working from a café and you don't want to be distracted by other customers and visitors in the café, choose a table next to a wall and sit facing the wall in the farthest corner of the café.
- If you don't want anyone to disturb you while you are working on an important project, put a Do Not Disturb signboard outside your cabin.
- If you want to drink more water, keep water bottles or glasses where you sit.

- If you want to avoid eating chips, biscuits and other unhealthy snacks, replace them with fruits and healthy snacks on your dining table.
- If you don't want to see your phone for the next forty-five minutes, keep it in a drawer away from you. If this doesn't work, keep it in a different room.
- If you don't want to switch on Netflix as soon as you get home, either cancel the Netflix subscription or keep the remote in a different room and keep your TV and home theatre system unplugged.
- If you don't want to do impulse shopping, you may delete Amazon, Flipkart or other e-commerce shopping mobile apps from your device. Don't save your passwords and credit card details on these platforms so that every time you need to buy anything, you need to login again and enter your credit card details again.

Please remember, doing your PDAs is your responsibility. If your environment plays a big role in determining whether you will actually do them or not, why not consciously design your environment that makes this easier? Things that matter the most should never be left at the mercy of luck or willpower. Don't try to win this war with willpower; use power rituals and a supportive environment. Remember the number one rule for building new habits is to make the behaviour you want to start to do repeatedly easy, attractive and rewarding.

Self-discipline is an act of cultivation.
It requires you to connect today's actions to tomorrow's results.
There is a season for sowing and a season for reaping.
Self-discipline helps you know which is which.
– Gary Ryan Blair

3. Daily Monitoring System

Another powerful tool in your success ecosystem arsenal which is often overlooked and laughed at is daily monitoring. Monitoring—not doing anything, just observing and noting it down has immense power. Remember the rule, whatever can be monitored, can be improved. If you cannot monitor it, or if you don't monitor it, how will you know if you are making progress at all? If you are not clear about whether you are making progress or not, you don't know whether to continue the journey or not. So monitoring is important.

If you have ever gone to a dietician for weight loss, the first thing they ask you to do is to buy a weighing scale and just write down your weight every day. If you go to a doctor with diabetes or vitamin deficiency, the first thing they ask you to do is to just keep monitoring the numbers. Same for your daily rituals.

Actively recognizing progress towards your goal
will ultimately end up inspiring you and have
you pushing even harder.
– Danzel J. Wellington

If you really want to make a difference, start monitoring your numbers every day. Decide your rituals with numbers, and then monitor that every day on your phone or a sheet of paper. You can do this on a Habit Tracker in a printed hard copy or on a mobile app. You can create your own daily PDA tracking system on any notebook also. We have printed Daily Habit Trackers in our **Dream to Reality in 5 Steps Journal & Workbook**.

Here are some of the examples of daily activities that people generally monitor depending on their PDAs:

- How many minutes of cardio/swimming did you do?
- How many push-ups did you do?
- Number of pages of a book you read
- Number of new cold calls you made
- Number of sales team meetings you conducted
- How many people attended your weekly hall meeting?
- Number of sales you closed
- Number of minutes you watched Netflix for
- Number of new people that joined your team
- Number of views you got on each Instagram reel
- Number of new YouTube followers everyday
- Number of subscribers you are adding to your email newsletter..., and much more

So decide what you are going to do. Do it with daily power rituals and monitor it every day.

If you are going to achieve excellence in big things, you develop the habit in little matters. Excellence is not an exception, it is a prevailing attitude.

– Colin Powell

4. Power Group

We have been hearing since childhood that our company determines our destiny. Our parents and teachers did everything they could to save us from bad company. Today, it is no more about drinking alcohol, smoking cigarettes, or not getting good grades. It is about our life and our dreams. We need to be very careful about who we spend time with. A power group is a set of people with we spend most of our time with. These are people who we brainstorm with on business ideas, challenges, new opportunities and strategies for rapid growth. The role of a power group in your career is akin to the role of your family in your personal life.

If you regularly spend time with five millionaires, you are sure to become the sixth one soon. If healthy eating habits and a good work-life balance are normal topics of discussion in your power group, you will naturally tend to manage your personal and work life well. If there are passionate discussions about huge growth, new opportunities, stretching one's limits and innovation, you too will automatically start thinking on the same lines.

One area where you need to have a non-negotiable highest standard is about whom you allow in your power group.

– Deepak Bajaj

It is a myth that if you're middle-class with a limited income, so you cannot be in a power group of millionaires. Remember the promise you made in Chapter Three of staying away from the EBC virus—No Excuse, No Blame and No Complaints. Being poor is only about less money in your bank; you can be rich in attitude, personality, ideas, passion, dreams and work ethic. These traits have nothing to do with one's bank balance.

Wherever you are and whatever you do, you can always find leaders and high dreamers in your industry who will value your company if you possess these core values. You only need to find these people. Also, the power group you have today will not remain the same for the rest of your life. As you keep evolving, your power group will also evolve in tandem.

But please remember, it is not about who you want in your power group; it is also about those people wanting to have you in their power group. So, you will not be in a power group you desire to be in, but in one with people similar to you. Also, you must yourself possess at least some of the qualities you want in your power group. Only then will you attract powerful people and powerful people will be attracted to you.

When deciding about who should be a part of your power group, remember these lines by Simon T Bailey who says, '*Expand your inner circle to include those who can challenge your thinking and escalate you to unreached heights of success.*' Your goal is simple. You should seek to join a group where the behaviour desired by you is regular behaviour.

If you have chosen the right power group, you may feel uncomfortable for the first few days. This is okay because growth is always out of your comfort zone, and whatever does not challenge you, will never change you. But gradually, conversations with the right people will have a profound effect on your conscious and subconscious mind, and make you a totally new person. I am super excited to hear your stories of your interactions and transformations with your power groups. Do share your thoughts, insights and transformations with me at support@deepakbajaj.biz or my Instagram account – coachdeepak.

You will never outperform your inner circle.

– John Wooden

5. Mentors in All Key Areas of Your life

Do you remember any instance from your school or college where you were not able to understand one concept despite all efforts by one teacher, but another teacher explained the same thing and you just got it instantly? Not only did you understand the concept at that time but also some of those concepts you had not forgotten to date. That is the power of the right teachers or mentors in our life.

Have you ever been to a gym and lifted weights with a trainer? If your capacity to lift is forty kilos, your trainer first encourages you to try and lift more, then without a warning, he quickly adds ten kilos of extra weight to the bar and signals you to lift it. All the while that you are trying to lift the extra weight, the trainer keeps his own arms braced under the bar, just to be on the safe side in case you aren't able to cope with the added weight. Had the trainer not pushed you, would you have dared to risk even ten per cent of the extra weight on your own? That is the role of the right mentor – to encourage us to take on more than what we think we are capable of, and to be by our side to encourage us to go that extra mile.

A mentor is someone who sees more talent and ability within you than you see in yourself and helps bring it out of you.

– Bob Proctor

During the school days, the right mentor was important for getting good grades in some particular subjects. But now you need mentors who can support you to design and achieve a great life and career. Hence, mentoring is absolutely essential today. A mentor can make a huge difference in your performance in every facet of your life. The right mentor can inspire you to dream more and achieve more. A mentor can foresee problems before they actually come up, helping you deal with tough situations. A good mentor can guide you to hidden opportunities.

Look for mentors who have practical experience, not those who pretend to be one after reading a few books. Go for mentors who are hands-on and have faced and resolved situations successfully. Also, one mentor cannot be equally apt for different areas of life. So, you must choose different mentors for honing different aspects of your personality. Your spiritual guru will not be the best choice for advice on financial or business-related matters. Your health coach will not be able to help you attain mastery on your emotions. I would advise that you find different mentors for different areas of your life in order to continue progressing. At times, your friends or family members can prove to be ideal mentors in some areas, and at times you need to look for professional experts in particular areas.

But as you begin working with a mentor, please remember that a mentor is only a consultant or a guide. He or she cannot do the work that you need to do. Your mentor can sit in the back seat, but you need to drive your car yourself. Also, mentoring is an ongoing process. Don't go to a mentor for one session of thirty minutes, and then return to the same old habit of blaming that mentor. Mentoring is a long-term process that needs regular course correction and adjustments. If you really want to grow big, plan to have one exhaustive session every month with your mentor.

Average players want to be left alone. Good players want to be coached. Great players want to be told the truth.

– Doc Rivers

6. Personal Evolution System

Be not afraid of growing slowly.
Be afraid of only standing still.
– Chinese Proverb

If there is one thing you should make a constant in your life, it is that there should be continuous growth. I strongly believe you are either growing or dying. If you want to grow, you need to design a system for your life and career that ensures you are growing continuously because growth doesn't happen by chance. Growth needs to be planned and meticulously executed. So it is absolutely essential to make a personal evolution system so that while you are busy chasing your dreams, your personal growth should not be neglected.

I personally love the word evolution which clearly illustrates that success is not a revolution, but it is an evolution. You cannot do something big one day and expect transformation, you need to work every day on small but important activities and then you gradually evolve not just from the outside but from deep within. As you start working on your personal evolution, please remember to include most, if not all, of the nine areas of good life that I have explained at length in the next chapter. The overlapping effect of one area on another may not be visible in the short term. But ultimately, they all work together and empower you to build your dream life.

We are what we repeatedly do. Excellence, then,
is not an act, but a habit.
– Aristotle

Here are a few things that should be an integral part of your personal evolution system

As the word suggests, evolution doesn't happen in one day, a week, or a month. If you truly want to evolve you need to ensure that you are regularly doing all these activities. Many times you read books or attend training events for new knowledge or skills. But if you are someone who has already read so many books, and has already attended multiple training events, you should still read more books and attend more training events to reinforce the good things that can totally change the trajectory of your growth.

One idea from a book or training workshop or your mentor can fast forward your life and career by many years. Remember repetition is the mother of all skills. Make these seven activities so much a part of your life that you don't have to make any extra effort to do any of these things. It should just happen automatically. Happy evolving.

Everyday do something that will inch you closer
to a better tomorrow.

– Doug Firebaugh

7. Monthly Growth Blueprint

Here is another game changer that probably ninety-nine people neglect. People are very good at making plans and taking action. But when it comes to analysing the results they are getting from those actions, only a rare few have this awareness to go back to their plans and review their performance vis-à-vis their original plan. If you can develop that system, you are in the league of the top few people in your industry.

Efficiency is doing things in the right way.
Effectiveness is choosing the right things to do.
Success happens when you are able to combine the two.

– Deepak Bajaj

No plans are perfect when they are made. Plans are made so that we start off with a broad direction and we know the immediate next steps. Plans give us the right beginning, but rewards don't come with just the right beginnings. Rewards are the results of completing the work in the right way, and that happens only when you constantly review and modify your plans. In that sense, planning and implementing is an iterative process that continuously happens in parallel. You do something, you get results. Based on the results you change the direction, take new actions, and continue adjusting the actions and directions till you achieve your goals.

As I have repeatedly mentioned in this book, something that is important should be included as part of the system. You need to make monthly reviews an integral part of your growth ecosystem. Once a month, you need to review the results of the actions you have taken, and do the necessary adjustments, and make a new Monthly Growth Blueprint for the next month. Just imagine where you will be after twelve such cycles of monthly blueprinting.

Let me illustrate the same through a formula called ACE

As the diagram suggests, the first step is to start doing

those chosen actions (PDAs) efficiently. It will empower you to achieve your goals. The second step is to maintain the consistency of doing those actions and the third step is to review the results of those actions by checking the effectiveness of those actions. After you have completed the third step, now with the new clarity, make necessary changes in the actions that we need to do, so that we can get better and faster results. And this ACE loop will continue and make you the ace player of your game.

The key goal of the ACE – Monthly Growth Blueprinting is the repetition of things that are giving results and the elimination of things that are not giving results, so that you get the highest return on the time invested. Please remember mistakes don't make you intelligent. It is what you learn from your mistakes that makes you intelligent. And you cannot learn until you review and analyse your actions. ACE will make you smarter month by month.

Productivity is never an accident. It is always a result of commitment to excellence, intelligent planning and focused effort.

– Paul J. Meyer

Key Lessons from Chapter 5 That You Should Never Forget

- Design an ecosystem for yourself so that success becomes automatic, continuous growth that happens naturally, and true fulfilment becomes an integral part of your life.
- Whatever is important should never be left to the mercy of willpower or chance. Convert them to rituals and practice them every day.
- The way you do one thing is the way you do everything.
- One big mistake people make while setting their PDAs or daily rituals is to overestimate what they can do in a day. Please remember to start with small actions. Build consistency, confidence, and self-belief by doing those actions consistently and then continue scaling up.
- You cannot achieve good habits without an empowering environment around you. Your space will either make it easier for you to consistently practice your good habits or it will make it a struggle.
- Whatever can be monitored, can be improved.
- One area where you need to have a non-negotiable highest standard is whom you allow in your power group.
- The key goal of the ACE Monthly Growth Blueprinting is the repetition of things that are giving results and the elimination of things that are not giving results so that you get the highest return on the time invested.

Exercises to Strengthen Your Learnings From Chapter 5

1. Evaluate all the seven Components of your Success Ecosystem and identify one or two areas where you need maximum improvement. Make an improvement plan and start work on the same.
2. Write down a few things that you want to include in your morning, day and night rituals. Be as specific as you can and answer four key questions about each of the rituals.
3. Complete your Creating My Own Heaven Today activity.
4. Carefully observe different spaces in your home and workplace and identify their impact on your activities and lifestyle. Design your spaces in such a way that doing desired behaviours and PDAs is easier for you.
5. Review your personal evolution system. What are the top three things that you have been doing consistently for your personal evolution? How satisfied are you with your personal evolution? Design your new personal evolution system for the next three months.

Detailed forms to complete these exercises are available in **Dream to Reality in 5 Steps – Journal & Workbook.**
You can get this from my website www.deepakbajaj.biz or by scanning the QR Code alongside. de.

Nine Key Areas of a Good Life

The biggest adventure you can take is to live
the life of your dreams.
– Oprah Winfrey

I was born and brought up in a family situation where money was scarce. Growing up my dream then was to attain financial abundance for my family. I chased money, corporate growth, and business success with a single-minded focus. I always worked with this philosophy of either This or That. While I did not discard my health and family totally, I definitely gave them second billing whenever there was more work at hand. I never realized that I could design a life with both, This and That.

Now, I have definitely achieved much more financial abundance than I expected, but I was lucky that I realized early in my journey that real success can be a combination of ever-growing career success, deep fulfillment, empowering relationships, and lasting impact. While I deeply respect the chase of big money, position, and social media followers, I know for sure that you can have it all, while maintaining good health, happiness, relationships, spiritual connection, and deep fulfillment. All you need is to fit this thought into your belief system and keep adding small actions to your daily schedule concerning all areas of life. Before you know it, you will start loving this new way of life.

The best way to accomplish this is by aiming for holistic progress in all nine key areas of life. I understand that life has different phases and in each of these phases, we need to prioritize and give more attention to some areas and postpone some of these areas. Hence, the priority and the time allocated to each of these nine key areas of life will never be the same every day or every month. But if you totally ignore some areas of your life in the name of achieving massive success in some other area, it will sooner or later start adversely affecting every other area and will sabotage your success and fulfilment.

Also please note that you don't need a particular amount of wealth, age, or position to successfully accomplish balanced growth in all these nine areas. All you need is awareness of how each of these areas is deeply connected to every other area of your life and a deep desire to achieve balanced growth in each of these areas. These nine key areas of a good life are demonstrated in the diagram below:

1. Health and Fitness

To keep the body in good health is a duty, otherwise we shall not be able to keep our minds strong and clear.
– Buddha

Good health is the foundation on which a good life can be built. A fit and healthy body will ensure that you look good, feel good, and do good work. The benefits of a healthy body always go beyond the body. When you are healthy, you have more energy, you can manage stress and pressure better and you have fewer chances of falling sick. There have been multiple studies that demonstrate that illness is the number one reason for absenteeism at work. Healthy people can work more and work better.

The only challenge in having a fit and healthy body is that you are the only one who needs to do all the work for your health. Nobody else can lift the dumbbells for you. Nobody else can eat nutritious food for you. This is one area of your life that you cannot delegate to others. Also, this is one area where results are not instant and there are no windfall gains. Your health is a reservoir that you need to constantly build.

With the new advances in medical science, access to supplements, and growing awareness of good health, we all will live a long life for sure. The only thing we need to decide is how we want to grow old. Taking care of our health will ensure that we will age gracefully and continue to enjoy and celebrate our life till our last breath.

Fundamentally you need to watch your food and movement to achieve optimal health and fitness levels. Eat healthy nutritious meals and avoid processed and junk food. Add forty-five to sixty minutes of workout to your daily routine and make physical movement a part of your lifestyle. You can do yoga, gym, running, swimming, cycling, Pilates or whatever form of workout you love, but working out daily is a must.

If you don't make time for exercise, you will probably have to make time for illness.

– Robin Sharma

It is sad, but true that we don't value anything till the time it is taken away from us. For most people until the age of forty, we don't see deterioration in health despite a not-so-healthy lifestyle. We all get a reservoir of good health and if we continue using it without replenishing it, one day it will be exhausted, and then we will start feeling the adverse effects of neglecting our health.

The biggest problem in making healthy choices is the delay in seeing the consequences of good or bad health choices. When you start following a healthy lifestyle, good effects are not visible instantly. So people don't get the motivation to stick with healthy habits. At the same time, when you are eating junk, neglecting your health and not doing any kind of exercise, their effect will also be visible only after a few months or years. This lack of instant symptoms makes people put health as their last priority. Remember, if you lose your health to make some extra money now, you will never get your health back even if you spend all that money on it.

Keeping your body healthy is an expression of gratitude to the whole cosmos – the trees, the clouds, everything.

– Thich Nhat Hanh

2. Spiritual Connection

When God is on your side, it really doesn't matter who is on the other side.

There is one cosmic superpower that is running this universe. Nothing is happening by accident. There must be something that keeps oceans, mountains, forests and the infinite number of people and other creatures together in a beautiful order. There is a supreme power that brought you and me into this world. But in our everyday lives, we get so busy maintaining all other relationships that we neglect our connection to our source, the ultimate creator.

You need to devote time every day to nourish and strenghten your spiritual connection with your creator. You can do it by some prayer, meditation techniques, or just by sitting silently with your consciousness. You can do it all by yourself, or if you feel you need some guru or mentor, you can take their guidance as well. You can do it with or without some music. You can do it with free guided meditations available on YouTube or try some mobile app. The most important part is to dedicate some of your time every day to nourish and strengthen your spiritual connection.

Irrespective of your religion or faith, I encourage you to devote time every day and be one with that superpower. Feel that power inside you. You are as much a part of this universe as much as this universe is a part of you. We all exist together in harmony and every dream will be fulfilled in harmony with the dreams of many others. Trust that power and remember life is happening for you and not to you. Be one with the universe. Surrender your goals to the Universe and continue moving forward with faith and acceptance.

As you deepen your connection to your source, you will feel more relaxed, calm and stronger. You will make better decisions, you will be more creative and your work will get a new grace and quality.

The ultimate goal of spiritual connection is to make you as happy in real life as you look on Instagram.
– Deepak Bajaj

3. Work and Career

Your work is going to fill a large part of your life, and the only way to be truly satisfied is to do what you believe is great work.
– Steve Jobs

Our work is an essential part of our daily life. We spend most of our waking hours at work. Hence, **if you are not feeling happy, intellectually stimulated, connected to your teammates, and aligned to your true values at your place of work, you cannot live a life of fulfilment.** In essence, your relationship to your work determines the quality of your life.

I started my professional career in 2003 at the bottom of the corporate ladder in the sales department of an automobile multinational company. I followed the core principles and rose to become one of the youngest regional managers at the age of twenty-five, leading a team of dealers and company executives as head of sales, marketing and operations for four states. I built a record-breaking direct selling business from the year 2007 to 2018 where I led a team of lakhs of independent direct sellers on a commission-income model. I started my own training and consulting company in the year 2018 and my social media and digital marketing company in January 2024.

All these years of working in different roles and different models have taught me that it is not the job or work we do that defines our success or happiness at work. It is the relationship we have with our work that determines our success and fulfilment. Irrespective of my role and responsibilities, I have been following certain principles that have brought me all the success and fulfilment at every stage of my career. I have shared the same six principles in the next few pages as key values to define your relationship with your work.

Choose a job you love, and you will never have to work a day in your life.
– Confucius

I have worked with countless people who are always frustrated despite making good money, and many others who are always happy at work and even worked extra hours even though their salary was not all that great. In my own companies, I have been seeing people who are happy from day one and are always excited to take up new challenges and responsibilities. At the same time, many others always look puzzled and stressed irrespective of how much money they make or the respect they get at work.

You can get KRAs from your boss but the quality of your work and the fulfilment you get from it is something you need to create. In the past few years, the percentage of people who are not satisfied with their work has been increasing at a rapid pace. It is not because opportunities are less; it is because people are not able to establish the right relationship with their work. Those who have good relationships with their work are the ones who will rise to the top of their organizations. Your relationship with your work is determined by the alignment of your values with your work. Here are some of the values that you can use to define and evaluate your relationship with your work. It is a list of qualities that will always keep you ahead in your career.

1. **Accountability** – If you have promised to do something, you will do it without reminders and you will do an excellent job of the same. If you are committed to delivering some sales, project, or report by a particular time of the day, you must honour your commitment. Every time you honour your commitment, your reputation goes up and every time you fail your commitment, you lose your good reputation. And you rise or fall in your career in direct proportion to your reputation.
2. **Solution provider and not the news narrator** – If sales are low, everyone knows it. You don't need to bring this news. What you should bring to the table is a deep insight into why the sales have been low and how can you bring it back. You need to be creative and find new solutions. Solution providers are the highest-paid people in any team. A few members of the team have one answer for everything and that would be, 'We are working on it.' Their work never gets completed. After working with lakhs of people, I have realized there are only two types of people in any team or organization; one who gives results and the other who gives excuses. So, never give excuses and if you have someone in your team who is always ready with excuses, replace them as soon as you can. How can you find creative solutions? Intention and commitment to continue finding solutions till you find one.
3. **Say yes to new opportunities** – Gone are those days when people join a company to do a particular job, and they continue doing the same till they retire. Rapidly changing customer habits and lifestyles

have made the work environment more dynamic than ever before. In this scenario, if you are not willing to learn more and do more, you will be the first one to be replaced.

Anytime there is a new opportunity related to your line of work, say 'Yes', and go for it. What factors decide a higher pay-package? Higher education or greater experience. You have already completed your education, but you can gain further experience when you try new things. Lakhs of people can have the same educational degree, but each one of them can gather their own unique experiences and enhance their value accordingly. Therefore, one should always be open to new opportunities.

If your actions inspire others to dream more, learn more, do more and become more, you are a leader.

– John Quincy Adams

4. **Always do more than what is expected** – For me, this has been the cornerstone of whatever I have achieved so far in my life. I have written about this in all my previous books also, and there is training workshop where I don't talk about this. I call it the power of extra:

   Do whatever is expected from you and do a little more.

   When you do more, you become more. When you do more, you add even more value. When you become more and you add more value, it is not possible that you will not be rewarded for the same. Delight your clients, prospects, teammates, family members and everyone you meet by doing more than what they expect. Make it a life philosophy to always do more than what is expected, and you are on the way to the top. Always deliver more value than your customers or peers expect. This little extra everyday will eventually compound to make you a dominant player in your industry.

> *You can start right where you stand and apply the habit of going the extra mile by rendering more service and better service than you are now being paid for.*
>
> – Napoleon Hill

5. **Expectation Management**– Unrealistic expectations are the number one reason for frustration and anger. When you don't get what you want, you tend to be angry and frustrated. But, in many of these cases, expectations themselves in the first place, are unrealistic and will never be fulfilled. So, if you operate with those expectations, you are bound to be miserable. Many people come to work loaded with expectations about everything at work—salary, timings, work days, work culture, colleagues, type of coffee, length of breaks, kind of work, type of boss, facilities at work, size of the workplace, design of your desk and what not. The bigger your list, the lesser your satisfaction.

   No place on earth can meet all these expectations. Probably, if there is any such place, will you meet their expectations? Once you have decided to work at a particular place, be grateful for whatever you have and keep working to make things better. If you are right, you can make slight changes in your work environment one by one.

You may expect a huge salary, bonus, or incentive. But if your organization is not paying you the same, please review your own performance in the last few months before blaming the organization for being unfair. I have seen so many people in jobs and businesses who expect more income every three to six months for the same work that they have been doing for many years. Isn't it wrong to expect that? At the same time, if you genuinely believe that you deserve more and the current organization is not rewarding you adequately, find a place where you are suitably rewarded for your work and make a move.

Every job is a self-portrait of the person who did it.
Autograph your work with excellence.
– Ted Key

Also please remember that you will not equally like every task in your job. Do not make it a condition that I will only do what I love. Your job or business comes to you like a package and you need to do everything. The majority of direct sellers or salespeople fail because they love talking to old customers or inbound calls. But they don't like to make calls to new prospects. I am an author and trainer. I love writing books, creating courses and delivering training programmes. But writing books or just creating courses is not enough. Being an entrepreneur, I need to manage sales, marketing, and other logistics to get more readers and course participants. Some tasks you will love to do and there will be some that you need to do. Just continue doing both in the best way possible.

When people are measuring what their seniors or organizations are giving them in exchange for their work, they often tend to ignore all the good, and focus only on what is missing. This attitude shows a lack of gratitude. The rule I personally follow is simple—first over-deliver and then ask for suitable rewards.

One big influencing factor on people's expectations is social media. When you constantly see a millionaire aged twenty-three or a unicorn in two years, a million-dollar income earner through affiliate marketing, and many other super-fast success stories, you just set your expectations based on that. Please remember, my friend. What you are seeing is only that part of this person's story that he or she wants the world to see; you don't know the full story. You don't know that person's struggles, resources, support system, opportunities and everything else that has led to that massive success. Don't make your opinions just by watching an Instagram post or reel. Get smarter and evaluate everything before believing it.

6. **Make your boss or senior irrelevant** – Do you want the rank, income or influence that your senior has? I can give you a guaranteed plan to get there. Do your work in such a way that you don't need your boss or senior to check your work. Excel every day and do everything the way your senior does. If you are doing what your seniors are doing, you will naturally be paid and respected the same way as your seniors. When I became regional manager in my company

at the age of twenty-five, with a work experience of only two years, this is exactly what I did to get that position. Nobody can hide the sun for long. If you are good, you will shine and rise to the top.

Whatever your life's work is, do it well.
A man should do his job so well that the living,
the dead, and the unborn could do it no better.

– Dr Martin Luther King Jr

As I conclude this section I would like to bring your attention to one term that I first heard a few years back. It is a beautiful new-age concept called entraployees. It is a combination of two words entrepreneur and employee. To me, this term conveys that irrespective of whether you are employed, or you are an entrepreneur, the fundamental qualities for success in your career, in both these cases, are the same.

In this new-age collaborative economy, if you want to succeed don't work with the old definition of an employee because the conditions in which those definitions were created are not existing any more. New-age concepts like work from home, bootstrap start-ups, crowd funding, collaborations, side hustles, drop shipping, freelancing, etc., are giving rise to new opportunities every day for those who are willing to work with core values of accountability, excellence and constant value addition. Continue excelling in what you do, and opportunities will come knocking at your door.

I tell people in their careers:
Look for growth. Look for the teams that are growing quickly.
Look for the companies that are doing well.
Look for a place where you feel that you can have a lot of impact.

– Sheryl Sandberg

4. Family

When everything goes to hell, the people who stand by you without flinching—they are your family.

– Jim Butcher

A family gives you stability, comfort, security, and hope. You always aspire to rule the world. Whether you make it happen or not, whether you succeed or fail, there is one place where you are always welcomed and you are the hero or heroine. That is your family.

My family is the backbone of everything I do. We stay in a joint family of eleven in one common house, and whatever we have been able to achieve is because of rock-solid family support. My family members are my cheer leaders, inspiration, support system and advisory board, all-in-one.

Like health, many of us tend to take our family for granted. A family is not just about the house you stay in. It is the bond that you share. It definitely starts with the bloodline or relationships that we inherit or make. But it is a daily commitment to nurture those bonds that make it a family.

Being a family means you are a part of something very wonderful. It means you will love and be loved for the rest of your life.

– Lisa Weed

Spend time with your family on a daily basis. Do things together. Eat together, have fun together, and create fixed timings or rituals when you do things together. These times will build happy memories and bonds that will stay forever.

Keep family first. Adjust and sacrifice if you have to but when it comes to family, make sure it comes before everything else. I am not recommending staying at home the whole day. I am actually against working from home. To me, work is work and home is home. I have worked from home for eleven years, and based on experience, I can say that there has to be a distinction between work life and home life. At some point, you should switch off work mode and switch on home mode.

It may not be possible to do this all the time. I have projects to deliver. I travel two or three times a week to speak at events and training workshops. But as a thumb rule, if I want a good quality of life, I should clearly know how to switch between work and home. I strongly believe in being in the present moment. So, when at work I am at work, and when I am at home or on vacation, I am totally at home or on vacation. This distinction brings harmony and balance to life.

A happy family life will keep you grounded and strong. It will help you manage stress better and empower you to take risks. Fulfilling family's dreams and making your family enjoy the best things in life serve as the biggest inspiration for me to work harder and take up new bigger challenges. Make your family your biggest strength. They are the ones who will celebrate every victory and share every failure. Many times you develop friendships that are as strong as your blood relatives and you can count them also as your family. Build bonds that last and relationships that empower you to do more and be more.

A happy family is but an earlier heaven.

– George Bernard Shaw

5. Intellect and Wisdom

Don't go through life, grow through life.
– Eric Butterworth

As you continue living your life and doing your work, never forget that constant growth and excellence are the greatest rewards of your journey. Money, rank and other things that you earn are really important but the most important is your personal growth. The greatest satisfaction comes when you look back proudly at your growth journey.

But growth is never automatic. You need to work for it through conscious effort and systems. I always tell this in my live events. Everyone grows old but only a rare few grow smarter and wiser. You don't have to do anything to grow old. Your clock will do it automatically. Your major role is to design your life and work in such a way that every month and every year you should become a better version of yourself.

Even before I started working in 2003, I had always asked myself these three most important questions; How can I do more? How can I do it better? And how can I do it faster? These questions empowered me to take up new challenging projects one after the other. Anytime I feel content, I remind myself of this one line my guruji always says, '*The question is not from where to here. The question that you need ask is from here to where?*' So, make it a life mission to constantly excel in whatever you are doing and aim to be the best in your field.

In a previous chapter in this book, I have outlined the entire seven-component model of building an ecosystem that can make continuous growth automatic for you. Follow that model and never stop growing.

The swiftest way to triple your success is to double your investment in personal development.
– Robin Sharma

Ever wondered why some people in every field get ten to fifty times more income or fees than the average fees or income in that industry? While most of the lawyers keep looking for work and charge Rs 1000 to Rs 10,000 per hearing, a few lawyers charge five to ten lakhs for the same hearing. Why some doctors are paid more fees for the same surgeries? While most of the trainers keep looking for work and are willing to work at any amount, some trainers charge ten lakhs or even fifty lakhs for one session. These are the people who have grown continuously and have been able to build their brands by constantly learning more, doing more, and delivering more value. So don't be just a face in the crowd. Become an industry leader and you can be the leader only when you make constant growth an integral part of your work philosophy.

Let me share with you a real-life example of what happened in one of my live events. One young participant came on stage and said, '*Deepak Sir, I am a big fan of yours. I got an amazing transformation from this five-day event and I announce today that within three years, I will be wherever you are today.*'

I appreciated the boy's confidence and courage and gave him my best wishes. But along with that, I told him something that came to me instantly, '*I appreciate that you will reach my level in three years. But what makes you believe that I will be staying where I am today after three years?*'

If you understand in depth, the statements from both of us are a testament to the life principle of continuous growth that me and my student both embody. Both the statements express our true conviction that none of us will remain at same level that we are at today, after 3 years A personal commitment to continuous growth will gradually build your brand in such a way that the best of opportunities will come to you automatically. Growing continuously is a beautiful journey and I really encourage you to start this for yourself today itself.

One can choose to go back towards safety or forward toward growth. Growth must be chosen again and again; fear must be overcome again and again.

– Abraham Maslow

6. Recreation and Rejuvenation

There is virtue in work and there is virtue in rest. Use both and overlook neither.

– Alan Cohen

Regular rest, recreation and rejuvenation are absolutely essential for sustained performance and continuous growth. You can neglect rest and recreation for some time, but after that, it will start adversely affecting your performance. If you are only in the game for a few weeks or months, you can do anything you want but if you want to work for a longer period with sustained energy and peak performance, you must plan periods of rest, recreation and rejuvenation so that when you are back to work you are ready to play your best game.

Many quotes on the social media will encourage you to sleep less and work day and night. At the same time, there will be posts and blogs that tell you to sleep eight hours in one single stretch, get a massage every week, work for only five days a week, and take an afternoon nap to enhance your performance. The best thing you can do is to test it for yourself. You have your own priorities, your own body clock, sleeping habits, eating patterns and deadlines to deliver. Try out what you think is right for you and see the results. The rule is simple: do more of what is working and do less of what is not working for you. The smartest thing you can do is to listen to your body.

I have personally observed that if you are resting well, you will fall ill less often. You will have more energy; your productivity and decision-making with be sharper; you will make fewer mistakes and handle stress better. Sometimes when you are on a break, you can look at your challenges differently and find creative solutions. Each one of us is unique, and what can be rejuvenating for one person, might be punishment for the other person. So find out what really rejuvenates you and include it regularly in your daily or monthly routines. We cannot fill from an empty vessel. So it is absolutely essential to keep our vessel full. In the pursuit of achieving your goals and serving the world, don't deplete all your personal resources. Refill them often so that you can continue serving the world for longer periods.

Life is all about balance. You don't always need to be getting stuff done. Sometimes it is perfectly okay and absolutely necessary to shut down, kick back and do nothing.

– Lori Deschene

7. Emotional Mastery

Self-control is strength. Calmness is mastery.
Don't let your mood shift because of the insignificant actions of others. Don't allow others to control the direction of your life. Don't allow your emotions to overpower your intelligence.

– Morgan Freeman

As per Dr Deepak Chopra, success in life can be defined as the continued expansion of happiness and the progressive realisation of worthy goals. Happiness and fulfilment are less about what we have and more about how we feel and think about what we have. Our happiness is determined by the meaning we give to what we have or don't have. Nothing is good or bad; it is all about our perspective.

The world around us operates with multiple forces working together. While most of what we get is not in our control, but how we choose to deal with it and what meaning we give to events happening in our lives is totally in our control. I strongly believe emotional mastery is being conscious of different emotions that we go through, and not let those temporary emotions affect our decisions and actions.

Feelings are just visitors let them come and go.

– Mooji

Anytime you are going through a tough situation, I want you to remind yourself that you have total control over how you feel about that situation. Anytime you are stormed by an array of thoughts, you should be able to remind yourself that you are not your thoughts. You are just having those thoughts right now. You should be able to question every thought and evaluate them objectively.

At the same time, emotional mastery is about not judging people or situations as good or bad. People are acting and talking based on their level of understanding and experience. They are going through certain situations and their words and actions are in alignment with what is happening in their life and not ours. We should forgive people and continue moving forward. Every action of people doesn't require your reaction. Learn to absorb things without reacting.

Also, please understand that correcting everyone is not your responsibility. You consciously choose your words, thoughts, and actions. Whenever in doubt, just shift your focus to your heart and seek guidance from your heart. Put all your trust in the universe, close your eyes, place one hand on your heart and ask for its guidance regarding the decision. Ask your heart about how to deal with some particular situation. Now just be aware of the sensation in your heart. If the decision you are about to make is good for you and everyone around you, you will feel peace and calm in your heart and if that decision is not right for you, you will feel some kind of discomfort in your heart. The Universe and entire cosmic power are with you. You just need to be aware of this power and look for signals.

What worries you, masters you.

– John Locke

Anytime you feel stuck, stressed and not able to think clearly, remind yourself of this formula called GAP

Pause everything you are doing and think about GAP.

G – Gratitude – Make a mental list or written list of everything that is going right in your life right now.

A – Accountability – Ask yourself if whatever is happening with you in the current situation, and how much of it, is in your control. Who and what has caused this? What can you do right now as the best step forward?

P – Perspective – Think about what could have gone worse in this situation. Go as wild as you can and think of everything that could have gone worse in the current situation.

This GAP exercise will not take more than five to ten minutes to do. But can instantly bring you total control of your emotions.

GAP Formula to regain control of your emotions in tough situations

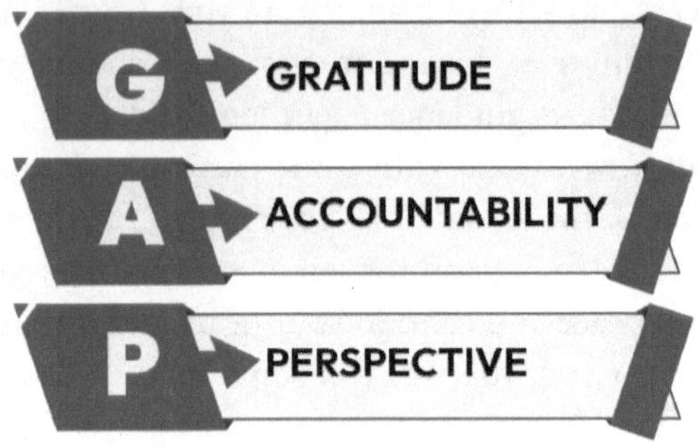

Life is measured in days and if you can manage your days well, you can manage your life well. The best way to manage your days is to control your emotions and not allow them to control your thoughts, actions, and decisions. Love yourself. Be kind to yourself and as much as you can, live your life in the present moment. Be, wherever you are. This journey of emotional mastery is actually about being aware of your emotions, gently shifting the meaning you give to those emotions, and navigating them consciously.

I have written more about emotional mastery in Chapter Three. You can read that part along with this one to continue your emotional mastery journey.

In order to complete our amazing life journey successfully, it is vital that we turn each and every dark tear into a pearl of wisdom and find a blessing in every curse.

– Anthon St. Maarten

8. Financial Abundance

The goal of financial abundance is to create a lifestyle where you and your family have the freedom to make choices without financial constraints.

– Deepak Bajaj

Money = Freedom

For many years in my life, my mom and I kept debating about whether we should spend our money to enjoy today, or whether we save the money to enjoy in the future. Both of us kept debating on this subject for years till I realized that actually the solution is not choosing any one of them; rather it is earning enough money so that we can spend today, and save for tomorrow as well. That is what financial freedom means to me—building wealth so that you can live your dreams today and save enough to meet the contingencies of the future. By the way, there is no limit on how much you might want to spend today and how much you would want to save for tomorrow. So you need to decide your limits on both. How I dealt with this puzzle is by saving and investing enough, so that I am easily able to maintain the lifestyle that I have today, even if my main current source of income stops.

If you follow the principles given in this book and if you are continuously growing and achieving excellence in whatever you are doing, you will definitely achieve financial abundance. Money follows excellence. So decide what kind of a life you want today and, in the future, and then follow the five steps given in this book to convert this dream into reality. If you put your heart and soul into this mission, you will definitely achieve it.

A big part of financial freedom is having your heart and mind free from worry about the what-ifs of life.
– Suze Orman

Here are some quick insights that can help you achieve financial abundance:

- Save every month.
- Invest smartly every month.
- Keep expanding your investment acumen.
- Use credit cards, only if you can handle it.
- Never take loans for luxuries.
- Never buy things to impress people. Shop for real value and utility.
- Never forget the goal is not to look rich but to be rich.
- Track your expenses and investments. Monitoring helps.
- Carefully evaluate big financial decisions like buying a home/car, foreign trips, big purchases, marriage expenses etc.
- Never upgrade your lifestyle as rapidly as your income rises. Rather increase your investments and repay your existing loans.
- Never compromise ethics to make an extra few thousand. Reputation and character rank way above the money in your bank account.
- Learn more, add more value to yourself, and be the best in your field so that you can earn more.
- When it comes to spending money, gather experiences and memories alongside gathering investments.

Aim for financial freedom and make a long-term plan for the same. Be grateful for everything you have while continuing to manifest what you want. Celebrate what you have and continue working for more. I have several videos for achieving financial abundance on: my YouTube Channel–**Deepak Bajaj**.

Wealth is the ability to fully experience life.
– Henry David Thoreau

9. Service and Contribution

People who are the most alive, driven, and fulfilled are those who seek to lead by a life of contribution and service to something greater than themselves.
– Tony Robbins

If you have ever debated the question of whether money can buy happiness or not, let me give you an answer that everyone will agree to. Money can definitely buy you happiness when you use that money to buy things for others. There is a different kind of joy that you get from serving others and contributing to the well-being of others, especially for those who cannot repay you.

If something can truly uplift your soul, elevate your self-esteem and give you confidence, it is the simple act of giving. Giving is very powerful. Make it your living philosophy to donate a part of your income and time to the service of others. If God has given you more than what you need, you should give it to those who don't have much. As the level of your income increases, increase the level of your contribution and service.

Serving and contributing to others gives your conscious and subconscious mind a strong message that you have so much abundance that you can share with others. Imagine your subconscious mind getting this powerful message repeatedly. How dramatically would it expand your self-esteem and mental blueprint?

The most truly generous persons are those who give silently without hope of praise or reward.
– Carol Ryrie Brink

As you start donating your time and money in the service of others, I recommend you do it so gently that it doesn't boost your ego, or make you arrogant. Anytime you give, be grateful for the opportunity to serve. Give with a full heart and in such a way that the receiver doesn't feel humiliated or low in receiving. Give without any expectations. Don't give to post on Instagram. Don't give because someone told you that if you give, it will come back to you, manifolds. Let the universe keep that account. You just give because you can and be ever grateful for the opportunity to serve and contribute. Give regularly. When you have more you give more, when you have less, you give whatever you can. Even if you can't contribute in terms of money, contribute with your time, but make service and contribution an integral part of your existence.

Giving to others is the greatest gift you can give yourself.
– Darren Hardy

Key Lessons from Chapter 6 That You Should Never Forget

- Real success can be defined as a combination of ever-growing career success, deep fulfillment, empowering relationships and lasting impact. The best way to accomplish this is by aiming for holistic progress in all nine key areas of life.
- The biggest problem in making healthy choices is the delay in seeing the consequences of good or bad choices.
- Nobody can hide the Sun for long. If you are good, you will shine and rise to the top.
- When God is on your side, it really doesn't matter who is on the other side.
- Everyone grows old, but only a rare few grow smarter and wiser.
- As you deepen your connection to universal energy, you will feel more stable, calmer, and stronger. You will make better decisions; you will be more creative; your work will get a new grace and quality.
- Anytime you feel stuck, stressed and not able to think clearly, remind yourself of the GAP formula – Gratitude, Accountability and Perspective.
- Make it your permanent life principle to always do more than what is expected and you will be on the way to the top. This little extra everyday will eventually compound to make you a dominant player in your industry and will also give you deep fulfilment.
- If God has given you more than what you need, you should give it to those who don't even have what they genuinely need. As the level of your income increases, increase the level of your contribution and service.
- The goal of financial abundance is to create a lifestyle where you and your family have the freedom to make choices without financial constraints.

Exercises to Strengthen Your Learnings From Chapter 6

1. Evaluate your life on all nine key areas of a good life on a scale of zero to ten, with zero being the lowest and ten being the highest. Identify areas where you are doing excellently and areas that need improvement. Pick up one or two areas of your life in which you want to excel in the next three to nine months and make a specific action plan for the same.
2. What is the one activity that you can add to your daily schedule to improve your health and spiritual connection?
3. What are a few of the things that you can add to your daily or weekly schedule to improve the quality of your family relationships?
4. What are some of the qualities or features that matter the most to you in your work? Evaluate your current work situation on those qualities or features. How can you align your current work to those qualities or features?

Scan here & go directly to my website

www.deepakbajaj.biz

Detailed forms to complete these exercises are available in **Dreams to Reality in 5 Steps – Journal & Workbook.**

You can get this from my website **www.deepakbajaj.biz** or by scanning the QR Code alongside.

Conclusion

This entire process of Five Steps from Dreams to Reality is in total alignment with how nature and the Universe also operate. If I explain the entire process with an example, it is exactly the same as how a seed becomes a tree and bears fruits. A seed is a potential; a seed is a dream; a seed can create a jungle. Every seed has that potential and every seed can become a tree. But only that seed which is picked by a farmer, who has faith in the potential of the seed and who is willing to do everything that is required for that seed to become a tree, will eventually become a tree. The farmer has absolute unwavering faith that the seed will become a tree in due course.

With this absolute faith, the farmer sows the seed in fertile soil he has meticulously prepared to give the right growth environment to it. He waters it, gives it all the nutrients it needs, clears weeds in the vicinity that are taking away resources reserved for it, and keeps a watch over it so that it does not get trampled over. He nurtures, guards and does whatever the seed needs to grow into a tree. When the seed is buried in the ground, nobody knows that it is in there. But the farmer continues watering it with total faith. He knows very well that he needs to do everything required of him, irrespective of the outcome. Even when no sign of growth is yet visible, he doesn't question his faith and doesn't start digging the ground to check if the seed has started sprouting roots or not.

Once the seedling sprouts, the farmer checks if it is growing as it should. He takes immediate corrective action if the growth is not as expected. If some insect or disease starts causing damage to it, he takes corrective measures. He knows that he has absolute control over what he does and zero control over what the result will be. He has a clear dream for the future, but all his attention is focused on the task presently at hand, and while performing all his duties, he remains emotionally detached from the results. The farmer also understands that there is a time gap between sowing and reaping, and there is a process that he needs to follow during this time period. When the time comes for harvesting the crop, the yield might fall into any one of these categories: exactly matching the expectation, rising above the expectation, or falling below the expectation.

In any of these cases, he learns his lessons, does more of what works and less of what does not work, and starts preparing for the next cycle of sowing and harvesting after selecting new seeds, with new dreams.

Furthermore, an intelligent farmer fully understands that every seed will not grow to be a plant, and is fine with it. A farmer never blames himself for seeds that die out. In fact, as the he gets smarter, he understands that every seed will not become a plant, and so, he plants more seeds than needed for the planned crop output, so that even if a certain quantum of seeds grows into plants, his target will still be achieved. At the same time; he realizes that when the yield comes out way better than expected, it is because of the Universe. This keeps him humble and keeps his focus entirely on achieving excellence in his process.

That is how nature operates. Have a dream, work with absolute faith and do everything you can to make that dream a reality. Make a plan and start from wherever you are and whatever you have. As you go along, keep improving on yourself so that you can do better, and do it faster. Be prepared for contingencies and keep doing course corrections as you go along.

When the time for results comes, accept the outcome wholeheartedly and review it to acquire new learnings. With these new learnings, new experiences, and new skills, go on to set up another dream for yourself and repeat the process with absolute faith. Every new dream will bring along new challenges and new learnings. It is when you completely and sincerely devote yourself to the pursuit of realizing your dreams that you will rise and unlock your true purpose in life.

This is the process that brings you success, abundance, happiness, and a deeper level of fulfilment. Your faith and attitude determine whether you take this entire process as a punishment or consider it a privilege. I can't wait to see you converting your dreams into reality. You can ask me questions during my social media live sessions or by messaging me on my various social media accounts or support@deepakbajaj.biz.

I very much look forward to hearing from you on your transformation challenges and success stories. Never forget that you have seeds of greatness within you. Your past does not decide your future. Today is the first day of the rest of your life. Never allow your inner light to dim. My best wishes to you all and your families.

May you not just write your dreams, but live your dreams.

Love, light, and strength. Keep shining!

Deepak Bajaj

Deepak Bajaj's Journey

The transformation of Deepak Bajaj from a shy village boy to a leading corporate trainer and life and business transformation coach, is a source of great inspiration and strength for everyone. Deepak has come a long way, and is a living proof of what can be achieved with clear vision, absolute faith, right values and untiring work.

Deepak was born in a family of government employees in a remote village in Haryana, India, and studied in different Hindi medium government schools. His father passed away after a two-year-long battle with cancer when Deepak was eight years old. Deepak had a tough childhood laden with financial challenges and many other difficulties. But all these years, Deepak grew up with one singular dream—that one day, he would become a 'big' man.

Determined to make it big, Deepak cleared the CAT exam and completed his MBA from a top-20 management institute. He started his corporate career in 2003, in the sales department of a leading automobile MNC and rose to the rank of regional manager in a record time, with the leading performance in the sales, marketing, distribution and operations departments of four states and union territories.

On 28 June 2007, Deepak started his first, part-time, side hustle in the direct selling industry, alongside his job. He resigned from his job within three months, to take up full-time entrepreneurship. Though excellent at sales, Deepak had no experience in building teams and managing business. He saw a few bursts of success, but could not sustain them, for the lack of a right team and proper systems. His business crashed to zero multiple times, putting his family through their worst financial crisis. It was a tough phase, and relatives and friends advised Deepak to return to a regular job. But he chose to work harder, learn more, and continued striding forward with the philosophy that whatever doesn't break you, makes you stronger.

He started learning the best success practices from across the globe. He read hundreds of books, did every online course possible and travelled around the world to get the best training from leaders of the concerned fields. The more he faced rejections, the more he invested time and money into his training and development. Gradually, he started creating his own unique programmes and systems, that had never been heard of in the industry. His perseverance and indomitable hunger for success eventually paid off, and he began setting new record upon new record in the field of direct selling in the country.

Deepak created several duplicable tools, training modules, systems and techniques that anyone could use anywhere to grow their businesses, irrespective of their age, background, location, education, gender or financial situation. Those systems and tools turned his business into an ever-growing passive income-generating enterprise. Millions of people from different walks of life have already fulfilled their dreams and established good, stable businesses using the tools and systems created by him.

On 10 June 2018, Deepak released his first book and started his own training and consultation company. The love and positive feedback that his first book generated inspired him to write more books. Subsequently, Deepak has authored three more bestselling books on achieving a dream life through direct selling. All four books have already been translated into nine languages, and are considered mandatory reading for those looking to succeed in this industry.

With more than two decades of experience in different roles and areas, Deepak is living his life mission of transforming people and scaling up businesses with his unique training programs, live workshops, motivational speeches, online courses, books, free video training and social media content. He is a master at designing and delivering customized training that brings lasting results and incredible transformations. He has already delivered training at 100+ companies and more than 2.1 million people from across the globe have attended his training workshops.

He has received the Best Trainer and Coach award multiple times. He has been featured in various magazines and has received various awards like Best Debut Author 2018, Best Entrepreneurship Trainer and Coach, etc. He has been a Josh Talks and TEDx speaker multiple times. He is also the brand representative of the E-Cell at IIT Bombay. He is an international master NLP practitioner and has received training from the world's best trainers and leaders in the USA, Singapore, Europe, Bangkok and India.

Deepak's live stadium events always run houseful because of their powerful international content, unique NLP-based methodology, activity-based interactive learning style and real-life tools and techniques that give instant results and lasting transformation to their participants.

He is a regular keynote speaker at various events, distributor meets, seminars, annual conventions, and leadership training programs. He is also a consultant to companies, helping them multiply their sales, performance, work culture and systems. People from all over the world consider Deepak's online courses to be the most affordable, trusted and fastest way to achieve results.

Deepak also runs a social media and digital marketing agency that helps people and companies elevate their social media brand, grow sales, run customer-centric digital marketing campaigns, build sales funnels and scale up businesses using automatic systems.

An avid reader, world traveller and adventure sports enthusiast, Deepak's life mission is to empower people to be the best they can be. He and his team have been constantly working on creating tools, online courses, and training events that can help people achieve their goals faster, and be happier.

You can connect with Deepak on various social media platforms and on www.deepakbajaj.biz

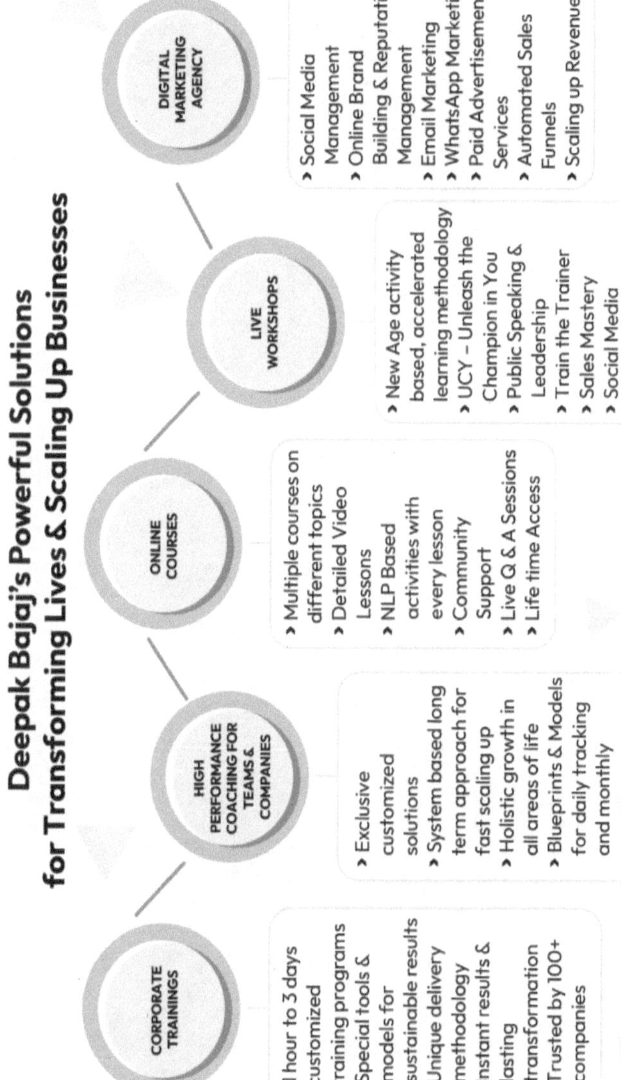
Deepak Bajaj's Powerful Solutions
for Transforming Lives & Scaling Up Businesses
CORPORATE TRAININGS
› 1 hour to 3 days customized training programs
› Special tools & models for sustainable results
› Unique delivery methodology
› Instant results & lasting transformation
› Trusted by 100+ companies
HIGH PERFORMANCE COACHING FOR TEAMS & COMPANIES
› Exclusive customized solutions
› System based long term approach for fast scaling up
› Holistic growth in all areas of life
› Blueprints & Models for daily tracking and monthly progress
ONLINE COURSES
› Multiple courses on different topics
› Detailed Video Lessons
› NLP Based activities with every lesson
› Community Support
› Live Q & A Sessions
› Life time Access
LIVE WORKSHOPS
› New Age activity based, accelerated learning methodology
› UCY – Unleash the Champion in You
› Public Speaking & Leadership
› Train the Trainer
› Sales Mastery
› Social Media Accelerator
DIGITAL MARKETING AGENCY
› Social Media Management
› Online Brand Building & Reputation Management
› Email Marketing
› WhatsApp Marketing
› Paid Advertisement Services
› Automated Sales Funnels
› Scaling up Revenue
Every next level of success demands a different version of you. Upgrade yourself & your team to Elevate your Success.

Acknowledgments

My sincere gratitude to each and every one of my readers, social media followers, workshop and event participants, coaching clients and teammates who have touched my life with your presence and wisdom. Every interaction with you has deeply impacted me and made me the person I am. I can never thank you enough for all your ever-growing love, support and prayers. This book is all yours. Thanks a lot.

I am blessed to have the best team on earth at my office. We have an awesome team at our company working tirelessly to develop new tools and techniques to make transformation easier and faster for people. Thank you so much for your invaluable contribution.

Behind everything I do, I have an incredible 24x7 support system—my family. I am lucky to have found my best friends, companions, partners, advisors, cheerleaders and my biggest supporters, all of these, in my family. I am nothing without all the love, care, support, affection and inspiration you all give me. Thank you, Papa, Mamma, Tanima, Gaurav, Divya, Saksham, Nirbhay, Prashansa, Cheeraayu and Devanshi.

www.ingramcontent.com/pod-product-compliance
Lightning Source LLC
La Vergne TN
LVHW090608110826
845146LV00001B/300

* 9 7 8 9 3 5 5 4 3 4 0 8 1 *